Successful Local Broadcast Sales

Paul Weyland

⏶AMACOM

American Management Association

New York • Atlanta • Brussels • Chicago • Mexico City • San Francisco
Shanghai • Tokyo • Toronto • Washington, D.C.

Special discounts on bulk quantities of AMACOM books are available to corporations, professional associations, and other organizations. For details, contact Special Sales Department, AMACOM, a division of American Management Association, 1601 Broadway, New York, NY 10019.
Tel.: 212-903-8316. Fax: 212-903-8083.
E-mail: specialsls@amanet.org
Website: www.amacombooks.org/go/specialsales
To view all AMACOM titles go to: www.amacombooks.org

This publication is designed to provide accurate and authoritative information in regard to the subject matter covered. It is sold with the understanding that the publisher is not engaged in rendering legal, accounting, or other professional service. If legal advice or other expert assistance is required, the services of a competent professional person should be sought.

Library of Congress Cataloging-in-Publication Data

Weyland, Paul.
    Successful local broadcast sales / Paul Weyland.
        p. cm.
    Includes index.
    ISBN-13: 978-0-8144-8053-3
    ISBN-10: 0-8144-8053-5
  1. Selling--Broadcast advertising.   2. Broadcast advertising.   I. Title.

    HF5439.B67W43 2008
    659.14068'8--dc22

                                                    2007021981

Printing number

10 9 8 7 6 5 4 3 2 1

Contents

Acknowledgments

This book is dedicated to all of those wonderful friends, relatives, clients, and broadcasters, without whom this book would never have been written. To Packer Jack Wallace and Rob Hunter for inspiring me to become a disc jockey. To programmer Dave West, who hired me for my first on-air job as an all-night disc jockey. To Jim Ray, who fired me from my first dj job, thank God. To Al Anderson, Jim Ribble, and Larry Todd, who taught me how to write for broadcast. To Ron Rogers, who gave me the opportunity to go into broadcast sales. To Lowry Mays and Dick Novik, for allowing me to manage stations in Europe. To Dick Oppenheimer and Ted Smith, for being friends and mentors. And finally, I would like to dedicate this book to my mother Shirley, my sister Valerie, and my wife Nancy for their love, support, and hard work.

Introduction

Since you're reading this book, I'm assuming that you are a media salesperson or you're thinking about becoming one. Perhaps you are a student considering broadcast sales as a career. Congratulations! Media sales can be an exciting and glamorous career if you know what you're doing. You get to hobnob with big shots and entertainment stars, and you may drive big, fancy cars. You could have access to the best tickets in town to everything from sporting events to concerts. You're invited to the best parties, and you may travel to exotic places. You acquire skills that allow you to work anywhere you'd like, even in foreign countries. You can make as much money as any credentialed professional person, including good doctors and lawyers, and you can do that without an advanced degree. That is, if you know what you're doing.

Unfortunately, there are many people in the media sales business who don't know what they're doing. Life for many of them is hard. Limited success turns to low self-esteem. Morale problems lead to fewer client calls, which mean even fewer sales. Fewer sales mean lower commissions and strained relationships with managers. Eventually most of these account executives either quit or get fired.

Turnover rate in radio and television sales departments is abysmally high and getting worse. Add that to other industry concerns like a languishing broadcast stock market, the downward trend in transactional (agency) business, declining market costs per spot, increasing demands for "added value" (free advertising), and an influx of new broadcast media competitors like iPOD, satellite radio, TiVo, interactive cell phones, and the Internet, and you'd wonder why anyone would really want to get involved in terrestrial broadcast sales to begin with. I'll tell you why. Because there is still tremendous opportunity for those who know how to look for it and harvest it. And that's what this book is about.

For the better part of two decades, we've moved away from building relationships with local direct business, instead focusing more on developing relationships with advertising agencies. In the process, we've sacrificed time and resources needed to properly educate and close long-term local direct clients. Particularly in medium and large markets, catering to media buyers and their agencies became our primary task. Many of us have learned, however, that our "friends" at the agencies can be fickle, stingy, and overbearingly demanding with their budgets.

Lately, this realization has led radio and television stations to put more emphasis back into building relationships with local direct clients. This makes logical sense because satisfied local direct clients offer less rate resistance and ask for less "added value." We have more control over local direct budgets than we do when we wrangle with the agencies. We have more control over the local client's marketing and advertising plan, we have much more control over the local client's creative process, and there are fewer revisions and cancellations than we experience with agencies.

In 1990 I received a letter from a former client who owned an office products store. He said he'd just sold his business to a national chain, and he just wanted to thank me for helping him become a millionaire. I shook the envelope to see if he'd written me a check, but there was no money, just the letter. That was okay. This client had paid me very well every month for many years as had many other business people who advertised on my station for decades. Many of these business owners are not only clients but also friends, who confide in me about every aspect of their business.

Unlike many of the new media, broadcast has a uniquely local advantage that provides local businesses with the perfect marketing and advertising vehicle for reaching out to local consumers. Simply put, local businesses and local broadcast stations are made for each other. Unfortunately there are two big problems keeping local direct clients from spending more advertising dollars with broadcast stations. The first problem is the client's perception that broadcast advertising is confusing, complicated, and a crapshoot. The second problem with local direct business is ourselves. Let me explain.

I think you'll agree that right or wrong, *perception* means everything. Many local clients are skeptical about broadcast advertising because they "tried us once and it didn't work," so naturally they think spending money with us is a crapshoot instead of a good, calculated risk. Clients are in the business of taking calculated risks, but understandably they do not like *gambling* with their hard-earned dollars, especially when they don't fully understand the rules. And the rules for using radio and television seem incredibly complicated to many business owners.

What is *reach*? What is *frequency*? What is *average quarter hour*? What are *gross rating points*? Why are rate cards so complicated? How much should broadcast advertising really *cost*? Why pay rate card when the next month the same station presents a special package at one-third the normal cost? How can virtually every station claim to be *number one*? Why does the client have his third representative from the same station in a year and a half? Clearly many clients feel comfortable investing with the newspaper or the Yellow Pages, and they are skeptical about broadcast, which leads us to the second reason we don't have more local direct business on our stations. And *we* are that problem.

Instead of making broadcast advertising look easy and logical, we have tried to sell with computer-generated proposals infested with terms and calculations that many of us in broadcasting don't even fully understand. Why do we inflict these complicated proposals on local clients? Why do we make broadcast advertising seem so confusing and complicated? Could the reason be because most of us don't know what we're doing because we got into broadcast sales completely by mistake? The answer is yes.

Nearly every single broadcast account executive I've ever met also got into the business by mistake. When you were 15 years old, I would doubt that you ever said, "When I grow up I want to be a salesperson at a radio or television station." Think about the bizarre, meandering path that your life had to take to get you into this business. I have. When I was 15, I wanted to be a drummer in a rock band. When that didn't work out, I wanted to be a disc jockey at a radio station. While working on-air, I became aware of the salespeople at the station. They seemed to come and go as they pleased. They dressed well, and they drove expensive cars. They went to lots of parties. I thought, "That's what I want to do." So I lobbied the general manager into letting me sell. I had to sell local direct because some of the people who worked at our station had been there for forty years, and they had all of the agency business locked up. I had no idea what I was doing at first and made every conceivable mistake. I wince now when I think of the early clients I would have served better had I known more about what I was doing with their money.

I, like you in all probability, entered into this business with very little or no experience in marketing and branding, no experience in the difference between good and bad advertising, and no experience in managing a business owner's expectations about results in an advertising campaign. Because I really didn't know anything my first year, I am certain that a lot of my early clients perceived me as a pest rather than a resource. When you combine a client's skepticism about radio and television advertising with media sales reps who don't know what they're doing, you wind up with a train wreck.

Even seasoned veterans in this business still don't really have a clue when it comes to properly educating local direct clients about the benefits of broadcast advertising. Many of us still don't know how to explain modern marketing and branding to clients in language they understand. We know as little about the creative process as the client does. Once the client determines that her sales rep is ignorant about how to make a good commercial, the "tail starts wagging the dog." The client, also ignorant about the difference between good and bad advertising, ends up telling us what needs to go into the commercial. And when the commercial doesn't work, who does the client blame? Your station, of course.

Speaking of the tail wagging the dog, let's discuss budgets. If, in the client's mind, he feels that working with us is more of a gamble than a good, calculated risk, why wouldn't he hold back on how much he spends with us? Why risk a lot when it doesn't look like the odds are clearly in his favor? Thin schedules combined with bad spots add up to a disastrous campaign. Add to that nasty formula the fact that most of us have no way of teaching clients how to calculate return on investment when they advertise with us. Consequently, the client may have unreal expectations about broadcast advertising results. And when those unreal expectations don't work out, the client cancels. And again, who does he blame? Your station.

By failing to contact, educate, and service direct clients properly, we are doing our local businesses a tremendous disservice as they are now in the fight for their lives against big box-store national competitors. All over the nation (and the world) consumers are drawn to rows of big, shiny, and flourishing national discount stores while local businesses are dying. The individuality of a local business has been lost in the bigger is better box-store craze. A shopping center in Austin looks like one in Indianapolis, or Portland, or Phoenix. Downtowns once populated with local retailers look like ghost towns. The national chains took away their customers. And with the customers went the money.

Surviving local businesses believe that in order to compete, they must match or beat the prices of the national chains. You see the evidence in local newspapers, Yellow Pages, and to a smaller degree on radio and television stations. "We'll match or beat any competitor's advertised price." "Buy one pair and the second pair is free." "Save 30 to 50 percent today only." Without even being asked, these local businesses are voluntarily giving away a huge percentage of profit in order to attract a few customers away from the national competitor. How long can this war last?

The price war is not a war that the local businesses can ultimately win. These businesses must have good marketing and advertising expertise or face extinction. They are quaking in the shadow of Darth Vader, and they need our help. The problem is, they don't recognize the help we could give them because we're not doing a very good job explaining it to them. In this book you'll learn innovative ways to help local clients that don't involve discounting their prices.

Just because we got into the broadcast sales business by mistake is no reason to be doing business by mistake. This book is the result of decades of experience working with local direct clients. It is designed to help instill good selling habits in new sellers and help them avoid frustrating pitfalls that waste time and effort. It is also designed to help experienced radio and television salespeople expedite the long-term local direct selling process, regardless of your geography, your market's economy, your market size, your ratings (or lack of them), your format, or your program.

The book is written in sections and covers virtually every aspect of prospecting, educating, and closing long-term clients. The first section deals with better ways to prospect for and then to get appointments with decision makers. We also deal with the disease of call reluctance and how to avoid it. I'll show you how to explain modern marketing and branding to a local direct client in language that he or she will absolutely understand and relate to. This section will include six very important concepts that you'll want to learn and include in every single local broadcast sales presentation that you do.

The first concept covers why broadcast advertising is easy, not difficult. We then go over a model of what a perfect business should look like in a perfect world, but how most businesses illogically spend the least amount of their time, money, and resources on the side of the business involving advertising. We discuss the difficulty that local businesses have competing with the thousands of other commercial impressions that are inflicted on a client's potential customer every day and how to break through that clutter. We'll cover how to explain the importance of branding to a client and how important that explanation becomes in selling the client on buying your station on a long-term basis. We'll also go over how consumers really listen to and watch radio and television commercials and why we're not trying to reach *everybody* during a campaign on your station. This concept will come in very handy as you work to manage your client's expectations about results on your station. It will also contribute to your ability to close long-term business with little or no rate resistance. Finally, in this section we'll see how your station is logical for the client regardless of whether you're rated number one or number twenty.

The second section deals primarily with the creative process. Here you will learn how to write genius creative regardless of whether you're a creative genius. These creative concepts alone will help you become a valuable resource in the client's mind. You'll study logical creative secrets that most agencies aren't even aware of to make your client's messages stand apart from the clutter. What you'll read in the creative section will also help you get more appointments with clients who are wasting their money with other advertising venues because you'll be able to prove that their advertising copy is inefficient and ineffective.

Then we will discuss how to help your clients calculate return on investment on the advertising they buy. This process will help you manage your client's expectations about results on your station, and it will be the final nail in your argument that advertising on your station is a good calculated risk, not a crapshoot. Explaining this ROI method to your clients will also help you to further establish yourself as an essential resource to your client's business.

Finally, we will cover the day-in day-out mechanics of the broadcast selling process, including better ways to make proposals and presentations. You will learn how to become a better negotiator, how to answer objections to radio or television advertising, how to overcome rate resistance, and how to close long-term local direct contracts. You will learn how to super-serve your local clients and how to handle collection problems. You will also find exercises at the end of each chapter to help you think about ways to apply each lesson to situations you encounter on a daily basis.

If you follow the advice presented in this book, you'll no doubt close more long-term local direct contracts. You will thrive in this business. Your income will increase exponentially. You will become an expert in identifying and solving customer problems, and you will gain a reputation as a resource. Your clients will love you for what you do for them. You will become as much a part of your client's lives as the other professional people they trust, like their doctors, lawyers, stock brokers, insurance agents, and tax consultants.

The one thing this book cannot do is change your personality or monitor how you spend your work time. Broadcast sellers possess various combinations of personality traits, but top billers generally have two traits in common—a strong competitive nature and empathy for others. The competitive nature fuels your drive to succeed. Empathy is the catalyst you need to help clients by understanding their unique situations and helping them identify and solve their problems.

To succeed, you must be competitive, and you must be willing to do the work. The most successful radio and television sellers average about thirty active accounts *on the air* in a given month. In order to get to that point, you must have long-term contracts. And in order to sell the long-term contracts, you'll have to get appointments and make presentations. Think about all of the local businesses in your signal coverage area that are not aware of who you are, what you do, or how to get in touch with you. How can they possibly do business with you or your station if they don't even know you exist? You must contact them because it is highly unlikely that they will contact you.

If you spend your time wisely and use your head, your efforts will pay off and you will be rewarded. If you're not busy, then you should be. There are so many clients out there who are not advertising with us simply because they're ignorant about how using radio or television properly could positively and permanently improve their businesses. And the only reason many of these businesses are ignorant about us is because we've never contacted and educated them properly. Or worse, they were contacted, but not by a broadcast salesperson who knew what he or she was doing.

Being busy is important, but don't confuse effort with production. The best part about beating your head against the wall is it feels so good when you stop. Too many of us waste time with spoiled, rate-contentious clients who won't buy us no matter how hard we try. Or, we find ourselves slipping into the rut of spending too much time in the office creating computer-generated proposals that nobody will ever read, instead of getting out on the street and properly educating clients in language they understand.

This book was written so that it is easy to read and easy to understand. The concepts have been simplified on purpose. We've tried the confusing and complicated way to communicate with clients, and it doesn't work very well. If you, as a media representative, clearly understand the concepts of how you and your station can help local businesses, then you'll become an evangelist about those concepts, and you'll explain them to every local businessperson you can find. As you explain them, you'll be amazed at how the client listens, asks intelligent questions, and takes good notes. Once clients are on the same page you're on, once you have clients who realize that you are a resource who helps them identify and solve marketing and advertising problems and not a pest like their other media salespeople, you'll have customers who will stick with you for a long, long time.

Enjoy the book. Use it wisely and build a rock-solid career in a really exciting business. Enjoy your position. Enjoy your time with clients and together let's put the *show* back into show business. Good luck and good selling!

PART

I

Selling Your Client on Why Your Station Is Logical to Buy, Regardless of Your Ratings or Program

CHAPTER

■■■ 1 ■■■

Prospecting Local Direct: The Key to a Successful Broadcast Career

How many new local direct prospects are you running on your station in an average week? If you're an average broadcast salesperson, the answer, unfortunately, is not very many. And one of the biggest reasons you're not running very many schedules for local direct clients is because you're not calling on them. When you do, you're not doing it effectively.

How can these local direct clients do business with you when they're not even thinking about who you are, what you do, and how to get in touch with you? They won't call you. You've got to call them. If you could just contact several of these local direct businesses per week, get appointments with them, and then educate them about the benefits of using your station to bring them more business, you could close more long-term business and make lots and lots of money. But first, you have to prospect.

Here's a little extra impetus to get you out prospecting more. Top billers in our industry average about thirty-two active accounts on the air in a given month. That's right, thirty-two active accounts on the air each month. These can be a mix of agency accounts and local direct or just local direct. Now I'm not talking about little two-spot-per-weekend accounts, I'm talking about thirty-two *average* accounts running on your station every month. Top billers all over this country are doing it. I did it. You can do it, too. The only way you're going to reach that high volume mark of thirty-two is to prospect your tail off, and then convert as many of those prospects into long-term advertisers as you can. This book will teach you how to do that.

SITUATION

Unfortunately, it's true that, with few exceptions, the average radio or television station will have fewer than fifty local direct accounts on the air in any given month. Even if you're in a rural area with a greater percentage of local direct business on the air, your station probably runs fewer than 100 local direct accounts in any given month.

Think about this: You're probably sitting on a gold mine in your community. How many local businesses do you have in your coverage area? Look at the business white pages in the telephone directories in your signal coverage area. How many businesses are there in your signal radius? How many local direct businesses do you have on the air in a given month? What percent of the total number of businesses in your signal coverage area does your monthly number represent? Chances are that in any given month you are reaching less than 1 percent of the businesses in your community.

While it is certainly true that not all of those businesses would advertise on your station, it is also true that a vast majority of them are advertising somewhere, they're just not advertising with *you*. If you need proof, take a look at the percentage of the businesses in your market that have signed long-term contracts with the Great Money-Sucking Hole we call the Yellow Pages. So, the Yellow Pages are successfully closing a vast majority of the businesses in your area compared to your point-something percent.

So, what's the problem? Why don't we have as many clients as other media, like the newspaper or the Yellow Pages? Could it be true that most local direct clients *perceive* that broadcast advertising is more complicated and confusing than print advertising? Could it also be true that local direct clients *perceive* that print advertising is more efficient and cost effective than broadcast advertising?

It is also true that a businessperson's perception will never change unless she is educated. And, it is unlikely that a business will ever be educated properly unless somebody who knows how to educate the client calls on her first.

OPPORTUNITY

There are hundreds, even thousands of businesses sitting out there right now that are not being prospected by your company. How can these companies ever do business with your station if they're not thinking of you as a vehicle for bringing more customers to their businesses? How difficult are you making it for these businesses to do business with you when you're not contacting them and then teaching them who you are, what you do, and how to get in touch with you?

We must never stop prospecting for new business. Business is everywhere, and new businesses are always coming into your market. Remember, new business won't just come to you. You will have to go out there and get it.

New sellers should be spending the majority of their time prospecting for new business. Veteran salespeople understand that because of account attrition, they too need to be prospecting for new business.

You must accept that *knowledge* about what goes on in the town where you work and live *is power* in this business. Knowledge means money for you. If you find out about a new piece of business first, you will claim it first, and chances are you will ultimately reap the benefits. Accept that there are literally hundreds or thousands of businesses out there who have no idea who you are, what you do, or how to get in touch with you, in every product and service category.

Most of these businesses are completely ignorant about issues concerning good marketing, good advertising, your station, and the right way to run a successful campaign. Your job is to find these accounts, learn everything you can about their business, and then educate them about yours.

Here are some great ways to out-prospect other media reps in your market:

1. **No one else is fishing in our lake.** Think of your station as a lake that contains thousands of fish. Other media, including the newspaper and the Yellow Pages, also represent lakes with fish in them. Think about product and service categories that are overrepresented in other media lakes and much underrepresented on yours. For example, take the service category of attorneys. It is highly likely that your Yellow Pages are loaded with advertising for divorce attorneys. How many divorce attorneys are advertising on your station? Is it possible that very few, if any, are running commercials with your company? You'll also find that many businesses in the same product or service category generally use the same media, usually print or Yellow Pages, but hardly ever broadcast. By pointing out that all of your potential client's competitors are "fishing on the same lake" and that your wonderful "lake" has virtually no one from that type of business advertising, you are saying that your client would practically have a monopoly advertising with you.

2. **Catbird seat.** In order to find out more about new businesses coming into your signal area and what they are up to, you must place yourself in some kind of "catbird seat." This means getting involved in your community, joining or creating organizations that would give you access to businesspeople and other advertising decision makers. Volunteer to help with area cook-offs and other local festivities. Join a Rotary Club or another service organization. Join your local chamber of commerce. Go to the business mixers, meet people, and pass out business cards. Visit merchant associations. These organizations are always looking for speakers. If you are so inclined, offer to speak to your group about the radio or television business. You might influence a decision maker and pick up a new account. I've picked up several choice accounts using this method.

3. **Leads groups.** Join or create an organization with other types of vendors who are all interested in learning as much as possible about new businesses coming into your market. If such an organization doesn't already exist, start one. Call a commercial realtor. Call someone who sells for a sign company. Call others who specialize in reaching out to businesses, such as someone in the office products industry, the printing industry, computer service/products industry, or other business services industries. Agree to meet for lunch one day per week and discuss what new businesses might be moving into your town and how to reach decision makers. Every once in a while, you'll get a real scoop on a new business or a radical change in an old business.

4. **Construction permits/utility turn-ons.** Go to your local municipality and see if you can get a copy of applications for commercial construction permits. Also, contact your local utility departments and find out whether there is a list of new electrical turn-ons available. Before construction ever begins, an electric line will be installed. I got the heads-up on many new businesses using this method.

5. **Go hunting.** When I began running radio stations in Europe, I made a habit of going "hunting" in groups of three to neighborhoods we rarely otherwise visited. Most of the businesses in these neighborhoods were previously "invisible" to most of our sales group. We would fan out and canvass those neighborhoods. We would visit stores and look around. We'd find all kinds of marketing problems and ways we could help solve them. Be sure to visit areas with road construction going on around them. You can help merchants in those areas that are under construction teach your listeners or viewers that those businesses are still open and offer more convenient routes to accommodate shoppers. On occasion, we found some real jewels of accounts using this method.

Store employees tend to be very helpful. When speaking with them, remember to always ask for the name of the person who buys the advertising. This is a very important point, because if you get the wrong person, then you're on a wild goose chase. Store employees may tell you what inventory is and isn't selling at their stores.

Hunting is a great way to prospect and to know what's going on in your community. Hunt every neighborhood until you are as familiar as a good cab driver with your community.

6. **Open your eyes.** Take the blinders off your eyes and ears. Take a closer look at the businesses you pass by each day driving to work and around your home that you just take for granted. Take another look at the businesses that you deal with personally but have never thought to ask about advertising with you. Make notes from the signs you see on cars and trucks. I got a big moving business account that nobody else in my market ever prospected just from calling the number I saw painted on the side of the truck.

7. **Prospect other media.** To me, it always did seem logical to monitor other stations and other media when I was looking for new business. After all, if a client is running on another station or media, it means that somebody else already did 75 percent of my work. Some other media salesperson has already convinced the client that broadcast advertising is a good calculated risk. All I have to do now is to reach that client and convince him that it would be in his best interest to also teach *our* audience, *our* thousands of consumers, who he is, what he does and how to get in touch with him. At times this parasitical method of prospecting worked for me. However, oftentimes it took months to get the client to switch stations or media, and to finally give me a try. Other times, I would find that the sales rep at the other station or media had not managed the client's expectations about results very well, leaving the client soured to using my medium or soured to advertising in general. Sometimes, I'd find that some knuckleheaded one-man-shop advertising agency was also prospecting the same way I was, and it would wind up with the new business.

In later chapters, as you learn the difference between good and bad advertising, you will discover that prospecting other media will take on a whole new meaning. You will find that you can take advantage of typical creative mistakes that local direct clients make when advertising in other media. You will be able to identify those mistakes and show the client effective ways to correct them.

BE ON THE LOOKOUT FOR NEW PROSPECTING IDEAS

Those were just a few great ways to out-prospect other media reps in your market. Keep some kind of recording device in your vehicle so that you don't forget the name and location of a business that you think you should call upon. If you think about it, it's really true: We really are sitting on a goldmine. It is also necessary to prospect intelligently. New sellers should spend a vast majority of their time looking for new business and meeting decision makers, not sitting in the office on the computer. Seasoned reps should understand that there is always at least a 20 percent market attrition rate in this business. That means that for one reason or another, 20 percent of the business disappears, and they should know that they too need to be prospecting for new business.

LOCAL DIRECT BUSINESS PRODUCT CATEGORIES

Try to come up with at least two businesses in each category that are not advertising on your station.

1. Air conditioning/Heating
2. Apartment
3. Appliance
4. Attorney
5. Audio/Stereo Retail
6. Auto Dealer, new
7. Auto Dealer, used
8. Auto Service
9. Auto Parts
10. Auto Body Shop
11. Bank/Financial
12. Beauty
13. Blinds/Window
14. Boats
15. Books/Magazines
16. Brake/Auto Repair
17. Bridal
18. Burglar/Security Alarms
19. Carpet/Flooring
20. Cellular Phone
21. Child Care Centers
22. Chiropractor

23. Church
24. Clothing, men, women, children, used
25. Clubs (nightclubs)
26. Computer Sales/Repair
27. Copier/Office Equipment
28. Dentist
29. Electric/Plumbing
30. Employment Services
31. Exercise/Fitness Equipment
32. Fence/Patio
33. Furniture
34. Golf Courses/Golf Supply
35. Hardware
36. Home Landscaping/ Maintenance
37. Home Renovation/ Remodel
38. Home Center
39. Home Theater
40. Hospital/Medical
41. Insurance Auto
42. Insurance Home/Business
43. Insurance/Life/Health
44. Internet Service Provider
45. Jeweler
46. Lawn/Garden Care
47. Language School
48. Lighting
49. Lingerie
50. Liquors
51. Locksmith
52. Lumber
53. Maid/Cleaning Service
54. Massage
55. Mattress/Bed
56. Mortgage
57. Motorcycles/Boats/ Snowmobiles
58. Movers
59. Musical Instruments and/or Lessons
60. Newpapers
61. Optical
62. Package Pick-up/Delivery
63. Painting
64. Pawnshop
65. Pest Control
66. Pet Sales/Supplies
67. Pet Shop, Grooming and/or Boarding
68. Pharmacy
69. Photo/Camera
70. Printers
71. Real Estate
72. Records/CDs
73. Rental Equipment
74. Restaurant
75. Roofing
76. Satellite/Cable
77. Sauna/Spa
78. Seasonal Recreation

79. Shoes	85. Travel
80. Storage	86. Tuxedo Rental
81. Swimming Pool	87. Vacuum Cleaners
82. Tax Accounting	88. Video
83. Telephone Systems	89. Wallpaper
84. Tire/Battery/Transmission	90. Water Purification

W o r k s h e e t: Prospecting Local Direct

Start developing a better system for prospecting new local direct business accounts.

1. Describe the prospecting method you used prior to this lesson.

2. Circle the percentage figure that best represents the work time you spend on prospecting for new local direct business.

   a. 80 percent   f. 30 percent

   b. 70 percent   g. 20 percent

   c. 60 percent   h. 10 percent

   d. 50 percent   i. Less than 10 percent

   e. 40 percent

3. About how many local direct businesses do you believe you prospect during an average week?

4. Name five local direct accounts that you are prospecting for long-term contracts right now.

   a. _____

   b. _____

    c. _____

    d. _____

    e. _____

5. In order of time spent, with 1 being the activity in which you spend most of your weekly work time and 5 being the least amount of time, rank the following activities in your average week.

    _____ Prospecting for new business

    _____ Writing proposals/working on ratings reports for clients

    _____ Working on creative for clients

    _____ Making presentations to clients

    _____ Servicing existing clients

6. Define one or more specific actions that you will take from this chapter and use in the next seven days.

CHAPTER
■■■ 2 ■■■

Using Media-Savvy Strategies to Get Appointments with Key Decision Makers

THE FIRST "CLOSE" YOU MUST MAKE IN THE SELLING PROCESS IS TO GET AN APPOINTMENT WITH YOUR CLIENT

One of the biggest problems in the broadcast sales business is getting the initial appointment with a prospect. The first words that come out of our mouths, either over the phone or in person, are critical to whether the client will allow us the opportunity to make a presentation. The purpose of this chapter is to discover better, more effective ways to "close" on getting more appointments.

They say the average person, including your client, is exposed to a minimum of 5,000 commercial impressions per day. Your sales call is just one out of those 5,000 impressions. Will your call stand out or will it only blend in with the other hundreds of impressions that your client is being exposed to in a single day?

BIG PROBLEM WHEN YOU "WING IT"

Getting more appointments is the first close you must make in the broadcast sales business. If you can't get an appointment, then how could you ever make a presentation and then ask for a contract?

Asking for the appointment is such a critical part of the sales process that there is no room for error and certainly no room for "winging it."

One day I had a huge revelation. I went to a department store and a clerk immediately walked up to me and said, "May I help you?" Immediately I said, "No, I'm just looking." And the salesperson walked away. Then I realized that the clerks at stores always use the same cliché openers, so it's easy to tell them the cliché answer and then watch them go away. You see? We all know this script when we visit a department store. Cliché openers for getting an appointment with your client aren't likely to be any more effective.

To get a meeting with a prospective client, you *must* use a headline to break through the clutter. Cliché openers such as, "I just wanted to take a few minutes to talk about your advertising" or "My name is ABC with station XYZ and I was wondering if I could come in and ask a few questions about your business" just don't cut it any more. The client has usually heard these kinds of noncompelling and uninteresting approaches from other media salespeople before. And it's *easy* to say no to a cliché opener.

CLICHÉ QUESTIONS BRING CLICHÉ ANSWERS

When I was in my first years in media sales, I felt very comfortable trying to get appointments with, "Hi, my name is Paul with KVET and I just called to talk to you about your advertising." But most of the time, I heard in response, "Well, we're not doing anything right now, but if you send us some information on your station, we'll get back with you."

And then, all encouraged, I'd send them all kinds of information on the station. But guess what? Nobody *ever* called me back. So, I changed my pitch to, "Hello, my name is Paul with KVET and I just wanted to see if I could visit you and learn more about your business." Well, the first time I tried that one, I tried it on precisely the wrong person. The client screamed in the phone, "IF ONE MORE MEDIA SALESPERSON CALLS ME AND SAYS THEY WANT ME

TO TELL THEM ABOUT MY BUSINESS, I'LL KILL MYSELF. IF YOU DON'T KNOW ANYTHING ABOUT MY BUSINESS, THEN I DON'T HAVE TIME TO TALK TO YOU!" And he hung up.

So, I went back to the old reliable,"Hi, my name is Paul and I just wanted to talk to you about your advertising." And the clients continued to brush me off.

Just because "it's the way we've always done it" does not necessarily mean it's the best way to do something. So, I re-evaluated the opening line I was using to get appointments and I realized that my opening line was just as clichéd as the one the clerks at the stores are using. I finally had to come up with something different and more effective to get appointments.

USE HEADLINES AS MORE EFFECTIVE OPENERS

A better, more logical way to get an appointment would be to use an immediate attention-getting device, just like we do when we write an effective spot. Think about it this way: Why do newspapers use headlines? To get your attention, right? It also makes logical sense to use headlines to break through the clutter and get your client's immediate attention. The things you say on your first call to a client are critical because you never get a second chance to make a first impression.

Here are some examples of headlines you might use to get more appointments with potential clients. Some of these "openers" will become much clearer as you continue working with the concepts in this book.

1. "I think I've figured out a way that you haven't thought about yet to get more qualified traffic into your store. Is there a good time this week when I could show you what I've discovered?"

2. "I have a great idea for a broadcast commercial for your company that could have a big impact on your revenues.

I've sketched it out and I'd love to show it to you. When would be a good time for me to come by?"

3. "I've learned a logical way to calculate return on investment on any advertising you do. It will make it much easier for you to track your newspaper, direct mail, any advertising you do. It will save you thousands in advertising costs, and I'd like to come by on Wednesday at 9:00 to show it to you."

4. "I've been studying your business and I think I've discovered a marketing problem with your store and a way to overcome it. Perhaps I'm overlooking something important, but if I'm not, I think I can quickly help you identify and fix a problem. When could I come by and show you what I've found?"

5. "I believe I've discovered a glaring weakness in (your client's competitor)'s advertising and marketing effort, and I have a logical way for you to quickly take advantage of it. What would be a good day to come and show you what I've learned?"

6. Here's my favorite way of getting an appointment—I love it because it almost always gets me in. "I (saw/read) your ad in the (Yellow Pages/newspaper etc.). That's a good medium. It's a big lake with lots of fish in it, but in your particular product/service category, wouldn't you agree that the Yellow Pages (newspaper, etc.) lake is being a little overfished? When people go there, they shop all of your competitors, too. On our big lake, we don't have one advertiser in your product/service category. Here you'd have practically a monopoly."

Obviously, most of these approaches assume that you've done some homework first and have actually learned something about your client's business. *Please make sure that you have actually done your research and that you have actually come up with a way where your client would really benefit from seeing you and hearing about your idea.*

It is logical that working on better headlines to get appointments will have a big impact on your ability to close more appointments. And remember, if you can't get an appointment, then you can't make a presentation. And, if you don't make presentations then you can't answer objections and close sales.

W o r k s h e e t: Using Media-Savvy Strategies to Get Appointments

Getting the initial appointment is half of the battle. Modify your opening line from a cliché to a provocative headline in order to break through the clutter and get an appointment.

1. Describe the biggest problem you have getting appointments with local direct clients.

2. Without fibbing, write down the typical opener you are currently using to get appointments with local direct clients. In other words, what are the first words you normally say to a brand new local direct client?

3. Out of ten telephone cold calls, how many client appointments are you currently getting?

4. In your own words, write down one single lesson you've learned from this chapter.

5. Name three cold calls for new local direct clients that you are planning this week and the types of approaches you'll use to get appointments.

CHAPTER

■■■ 3 ■■■

Making Broadcast Advertising User-Friendly

This chapter is the first in a series of concepts about how to explain marketing and branding to local direct clients. Make absolutely certain you understand all of the following six concepts and can recite them during presentations to direct clients. If you think these concepts are too simple, believe me, you're wrong. I've dealt with literally thousands of local direct clients, taken them through this presentation, and not one time have I ever heard, "Oh, I know all of that," because they don't.

At a recent National Association of Broadcasters meeting for television, managers had the opportunity to visit with a panel of automobile dealers. One of the television managers asked the panel what broadcasters could do to make dealers' lives easier. One of the dealers responded with, "Well, I guess I need to learn more about Cost Per Point. That really confuses me . . . heck, I guess I just need to hire an advertising agency." "Oh no," I thought.

Another manager asked the same dealer, "What are we doing right?" The dealer quickly said, "I love Dave Smith's tv station. They seem to know what they're doing. I go there every week to cut spots and Dave always makes me feel welcome and at home."

So, what is the dealer really saying? He'd rather hire an agency than deal with complicated broadcast ratings formulas. And, what he's really looking for is a relationship with someone he trusts and makes him feel comfortable.

Our industry has made what we do for a living seem much more complicated than it really is. As a result, most local direct clients think that buying radio or television schedules is difficult, confusing, and expensive. Whose fault is it that clients feel this way about our product? It's our fault as an industry. Let's look at how local businesses perceive our industry and how we can begin to change that perception.

It's hard to win a game when you don't know the rules. That's why it is in our best interest to educate clients about the benefits of broadcast advertising, but in language the client understands, not in our ratings-oriented mumbo-jumbo. If more of our salespeople simply realized that it's hard for clients to buy something they don't understand, and that educated clients buy more than uneducated clients, logically our total share of local direct revenues would be much, much larger. Rate resistance, losing clients to agencies, and reluctance to sign long-term contracts are usually symptoms of client ignorance. Remember, it's hard to buy into something when you don't perceive its value.

By focusing your attention on educating the client in language that he or she would understand, you can do several wonderful things.

1. Eliminate rate resistance.
2. Eliminate requests for freebies or other "added value."
3. Make the sale whether your station is rated number one or number twenty.
4. Double or triple what your client believes he or she should spend on your station.
5. Get a long-term contract.

In order to do these things, we must change the way we talk to our clients. It's time to make things easier, not harder. We need to back away from the complicated ratings-oriented talk we've been inflicting on clients for the past thirty-some-odd years and go back to what made us successful with local direct clients in the first place: simple logic and easier explanations about how and why businesses should use broadcast advertising.

WHAT BUSINESS OWNERS KNOW ABOUT ADVERTISING

Let's begin with the premise that most business owners know very little about marketing, advertising, or how to use broadcast effectively. This is actually a fact, not an assumption. It's not that they are stupid, it's just that, generally, people are ignorant about these subjects. Consequently, people are naturally skeptical about buying something they're not familiar with.

For example, all of us have had a client who said, "I tried radio (or tv) and it didn't work." That is a statement of ignorance. All forms of media "work." All media are good. Television is good. Radio is good. Newspaper and the Yellow Pages are all good. But they must be used properly in order to achieve a measurable result.

DON'T BE A CHIQUITA

It's not just the clients who have the ignorance problem. There is a second reason that we have a problem selling and retaining local direct business, and that problem is all of us in the broadcast business. Just how difficult are *you* making it for local direct clients to do business with you and your station?

I work in Mexico City regularly doing seminars on broadcast selling. Once I held an event in Chapultapec, a very rich part of Mexico City. And those of you who have been to Mexico City know that if you're rich in Mexico, you're *rich*. But even in that very wealthy part of the city, there were signs of abject poverty everywhere.

On virtually every street corner there were little girls with grubby faces that the locals called "chiquitas." They hold out their hands and beg every passer-by for money, and they have nothing to offer in return. "Por favor, señor . . . just a little something," they ask. You respond, "No, chiquita, not today. This begging is very dangerous. Don't do this." But the chiquitas are very persistent. "Por favor . . . just a little something for me . . . *por favor.*"

Obviously, this kind of poverty is very sad. Sometimes, though, broadcast salespeople remind me of them. "Por favor, Mr. Client. Just a little something for my station, por favor." And the client says, "No, chiquita, not today. But if you send me some information on your station, I'll get right back with you." And the chiquita salesperson says enthusiastically, "Okay, I'll get you some information right to you."

Then the chiquita runs back to the station, cards the account, then gets on the computer and cranks out a computerized proposal filled with horrible stuff that nobody likes to read or can understand, like average quarter hour (AQH) and cost per point (CPP) and Frequency of 3. You get all of that stuff to your client, and then of course, the client never calls you back. If I were a local direct client who already had the perception that broadcast advertising was complicated, confusing, and expensive, I believe I'd rather chew on a mouthful of wasps than try to read one more computer-generated report or package from a radio or television station.

See, here's the problem—and the opportunity. The average radio or television station has fewer than fifty local direct accounts on the air in any given month. Meanwhile, another medium out there has practically every single account, thousands of them, locked up with annual contracts. That medium is the Yellow Pages. It's not that all of those local advertisers aren't advertising; they're just not advertising with YOU. Why? Because of the way we sell. We're an industry of chiquitas, and we end up giving local direct clients facts and figures that even WE don't fully understand. So, how should we expect anybody else to understand them?

Here's a great test. Explain GRPs, AQH, and frequency to your mom, in language that she would understand that would get her excited and ready to buy from you before her eyes turn yellow and cross. It's not an easy thing to do. So, why keep going there with clients? These computer-generated reports are not good for educating local direct clients. All they do is fuel the argument that broadcast advertising is confusing and complicated.

The best part about beating your head against a wall is that it feels so good when you stop. Stop confusing and boring your clients with nonsense ratings proposals they don't understand. Stop confusing effort with production. Stop being chiquitas, begging clients for money without offering anything valuable in return. And what do I mean by "value"? I mean identifying and solving client problems, but more on that later.

While I was in college, I worked at a local campus men's store. Often people who came into our store were chiquitas who were trying to sell us something. And all of the chiquitas who visited us would say the same, cliché things:

- We're number *one*.
- We've got a 3.2.
- We have the *biggest stick in town*.
- Oh, you'll *love* our morning show!
- I just need to make *one more sale* and I get to go to *Jamaica* with our station!
- Don't buy that station over there . . . the people who listen to *that* station live on *the street and smoke crack!*

Not one single media salesperson ever came in and spoke to us in language that we understood, about how it would be logical and in our best interest to do business with them.

We know that educated clients buy more than uneducated clients. We know that our local direct clients have been inundated with chiquitas from every media and every station. (Clients hate chiquitas and would do almost anything to get rid of them.) And, instead of educating clients properly about good marketing, the difference between good and bad advertising and how to calculate return on investment on the advertising they're doing, all the chiquita has to offer is a report written in crapola hieroglyphics that nobody can or wants to read. All the chiquita can do is a little chest-beating dance about how his or her station is number one with 24- to 49-year-old women who shave one eyebrow and drive Lincolns.

The broadcast industry has a marketing problem with local direct advertisers. It's that pesky perception that what we do for a living is confusing, complicated, and expensive. Instead of perceiving us as resources, we look like pests. Instead of having a knowledgeable marketing and advertising expert to help them grow their businesses, they get to meet their third chiquita in a year and a half from your station. It's a shame, but that's what local direct clients think about broadcast advertising—that is, if they even bother to think about using us at all. And guess what? We have nobody to blame but ourselves.

and somehow not trust-worthy

LESSONS FROM OTHER INDUSTRIES

Let's look other industries and try to understand how difficult they made it for people to do business with them. Have you tried to buy a mobile phone lately? How about a digital camera? An HD tv? A lot of people are intimidated by high-tech gadgetry. There seem to be so many options on features and brands. With phones, look at all of the confusing calling plans.

With computer security problems as bad as they are, what do you really know about different firewalls, operating systems, and Internet service providers and the options that they do or don't provide? Many of us had certain fears and perceptions about PCs that kept us from buying them when they first appeared on store shelves. The choices now are even more complicated. And instead of educating us in language that we could easily understand, many of these industries continue to talk down to us. How difficult are these companies making it for us to buy from them, when the choices, benefits, and results aren't crystal clear? Are these companies really identifying and solving your problems in language that is easy for you to understand? No.

Aren't these companies taking huge risks by assuming that the average consumer knows everything they know? Many people perceive that these new electronic devices are expensive. The fact is, though, that many of the new phones and other devices are now so inexpensive that it probably makes sense to switch them out every year or so. It's too bad that potential consumers are so intimidated that they hang onto the same old workhorse device for years, or until they are completely obsolete.

So whose fault is it that millions of consumers are ignorant about the benefits and results that these new mobile phones, computers, PDAs, and other digital gadgets could bring us? It's the companies' fault. If they bothered to *educate* us in language that we could easily understand, we'd probably purchase more of these items in a more timely fashion. In other words, if we were better educated about some of these products, we'd probably be spending more money on them.

TAKE RESPONSIBILITY FOR THE EDUCATION OF YOUR CLIENTS

The broadcast business is no different. Keep in mind that most people outside of the media industry and advertising agency business have no idea how the broadcast advertising process works.

ADVERTISING IS EASY

In order to educate local direct clients correctly, we must begin by disarming them. We've got to let them know that what we do for a living is not complicated. In fact, it's very simple. Our job is basically this: *to teach our thousands of listeners or viewers WHO the client is, WHAT the client does, and HOW to get in touch with the client.* How hard is that?

Help your client to think that what we do is very easy. Tell him or her that you are simply a broker for a huge group of consumers with eyes and ears and legs and wallets. Tell the client that you represent a lake containing thousands of fish. At any given moment, many of those fish are coming toward the surface to feed. It makes sense that if these fish are hungry for what the client is selling, if the bait is attractive enough, and if we cast the line enough times so that the bait becomes familiar, then it seems like a logical calculated risk that your client will catch fish on your lake.

W o r k s h e e t: Making Broadcast Advertising User-Friendly

Let local direct clients know that what we do for a living is not complicated. In fact, it's very simple.

1. Our job as media salespeople is not difficult, but we've made it seem hard. In your own words, write a sentence or two explaining how easy your job in broadcast sales really is.

2. How could you more easily explain your services to a local direct client?

3. Define one or more specific actions that you will take from this chapter and use in the next seven days.

CHAPTER

■■■ 4 ■■■

Explaining Broadcast Marketing to a Direct Client

Branding:
Building an
image in the
customer's mind
that is distinct
and discernable
from the competition.

Think of marketing as the entire effort a client makes to provide a product or service to consumers. Marketing would include the client's concept, pricing, packaging, and location. Marketing would include the client's sales force. And, marketing would also include the client's advertising strategy. Although advertising is a very important part of the overall marketing process, it's often the part that's the least understood.

ADVERTISING IS A MYSTERY TO MOST CLIENTS

If a business in your signal coverage area is even thinking of your station at all as an advertising venue, where do you think he's coming up with the budget that he's willing to "gamble" with you? Let's face it—most businesses perceive that advertising is an uncertainty. Many business owners actually believe that advertising is a complete waste of money. So when a client is planning her budget for marketing her business, how is she coming up with the amount she's willing to invest in advertising? Is it possible that most clients pull that number right out of thin air? Absolutely.

For most clients, advertising is the most mysterious part of business. It is often the most difficult business expenditure to justify. For many businesses, broadcast advertising is an intangible concept like insurance. You can't touch it, it's not tangible, so broadcast advertising is usually the hardest part of the budget to qualify and quantify. It's voodoo. That's why when business gets tough, the first thing that gets nixed is advertising. This of course, is completely illogical. Imagine a CEO talking to shareholders, "Oh, the economy is getting soft! So, the first thing we'll do is stop teaching people who we are, what we do, and how to get in touch with us."

This is a mistake. How difficult is a client making it for people to do business with him if they don't know who he is, what he does, or how to get in touch with him? Advertising is fully one-third of the importance of the health of any business. Here is a wonderful way to show a client, in language that she will understand, how important advertising is to her entire business strategy. Draw an equilateral triangle on a piece of paper. An equilateral triangle is a triangle with three equal sides. On the left side of the triangle, write **Product/Service**. On the right side write **Sales Force**. On the bottom, write **Advertising**.

Advertising *NAME RECOGNITION*

Point out the following, using the pyramid with the labeled sides, to the client. What if, for example, you have a great product or service, great advertising, and no sales force? Your business would be in trouble, no question about it. If you had a great sales force and good advertising, but the product or service was poorly conceived or poorly priced or badly packaged or not available, then the business would also be in trouble.

And what if you had a good product or service, and a good sales force, but no advertising? How difficult would you be making it for people to do business with you if they didn't know who you were, what you do, or how to get in touch with you?

In a perfect business, all three sides of the triangle are equal. A business can only be successfully marketed if advertising is treated as equally important as its product/service and sales force. Ask your client, "What does your marketing triangle look like?" I'll bet it's far from looking like a perfect pyramid. Most clients' marketing triangles look more like a witch hat than an equilateral triangle. And the side that says advertising is usually the weakest link

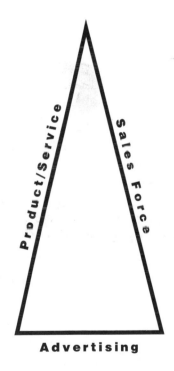

INVISIBILITY

How invisible is your client's business? Have you ever had the experience of driving the same route to work every single day and then one day noticing a new building in the last stages of construction?

"Where in the heck did that come from?" you might ask. "Why didn't I notice that before?" Somehow to you, that construction project might as well have been wearing an invisible cloak.

A friend of mine owns a jewelry store. He is constantly frustrated about losing business to big box-stores. He doesn't understand why people would buy anywhere else but from him. He is convinced that he offers finer merchandise at better prices than his competitors, and perhaps he does. He has very little faith in the advertising process and is bull-headed in his idea that just because he built it, "they will come." What he can't see is that in this over-cluttered world, his store is becoming increasingly overlooked and even invisible to consumers. It is possible that soon he'll join the thousands of other local direct clients that have been driven out of business by huge out-of-town competitors.

We must explain to our clients that logically and statistically, provided their business isn't seasonal (like selling Christmas trees) and doesn't have marketing problems, a percentage of the viewers or listeners in your signal coverage area *will* buy what your client is selling, either from her or one of her competitors this week. The question becomes, how can these consumers even consider buying from your client when they are not even thinking about who she is, what she does, or how to get in touch with her? Just how invisible is your client to your audience? *The audience (customers) is there.*

ADVERTISING WILL NOT CURE MARKETING PROBLEMS

At this point, remind the client that even the best advertising campaign in the world cannot help a client with marketing problems. Advertising a business with marketing problems is like putting lipstick on a pig. In other words, good advertising will not cure a business if the product or service is poorly conceived, overpriced, hard to locate, or not easily available. *Or has no market.*

It is very important for the media salesperson to identify marketing problems and to ask the client questions about them **before** a campaign begins. Remember, if the client's product or service

PROBLEM QUESTIONS.

doesn't make any sense to you, then how would you explain it to your listeners or viewers? For example, it would make very little sense to advertise a smoke alarm with a snooze feature. Or, what if an adult diaper came out with a new thong model? If the product or service is flawed and you don't point it out, chances are the client will eventually blame your medium when his advertising campaign "didn't work." If you suspect that your client has marketing problems, act like a detective and ask questions. Here is an example of what can happen when a media salesperson doesn't point out obvious marketing problems early on to a client. I had a friend who was ready to advertise his new Internet site. He'd spent a considerable amount of money trying to consolidate the promotional products business all at one big Internet address. The problem was that his business model was so confusing and complicated that he couldn't easily explain it to me or to his potential clients. In fact, I asked him point blank to explain to me in under two minutes how his business worked and how people would benefit by hiring him, and he couldn't do it. But my friend still hired an advertising agency and ran a big advertising campaign anyway. Nothing in the campaign made his business any easier to understand. When the campaign didn't work, guess who he blamed? The media he used. He's not alone in blaming a specific medium for failure. Many businesses advertise and still fail as a result of hare-brained ideas, poor locations, rude employees, bad pricing, and the like. Blaming the media they used makes more sense than blaming themselves for a marketing problem.

On several occasions I have chosen not to take a client's money, even though that client was eager to spend it with me. In one case in Geneva, Swizerland, a client called the station and wanted to advertise a very unique kind of jewelry. We arranged a meeting, and he excitedly opened a polished wooden box containing crystal amulets filled with colored liquid and what appeared to be floating snot. I asked him what it was and he said, "It's pure DNA. I have developed a process in which I can get your DNA inside of a piece of jewelry. You can wear it as a pendant or even earrings."

"Wow," I replied. "How do you get the DNA?"

"Easily," he said. "I just take a piece of your flesh." Thinking I had misunderstood him because of his heavy French accent, I repeated the question. "Yes," he said again, "I use this device and take a piece of your flesh." He then showed me a sterile syringe-looking instrument that looked like something out of a science-fiction film. It had sharp little grabbers on the end. "Wouldn't that cause bleeding?" I asked. "Of course," he said. "So you apply this bandage and the bleeding stops," he responded. As a test, I asked him to explain the procedure to several of the station's employees, many of whom had several facial piercings. After wincing in horror, every single one of them said they would not be interested in DNA jewelry, particularly after they learned the cost. He wanted roughly $500 for a pendant, along with a piece of your hide, literally. The client finally realized that even advertising wouldn't help sell his freaky product.

So you see? Even a great advertising campaign cannot help a client with severe marketing problems. Use the marketing pyramid model to help draw out potential product or service problems before a campaign begins. You might be able to help your client overcome problems that are not obvious.

SHOW THE TRIANGLE TO CLIENTS

Show the triangle to your clients. It's good for two things. First, you're teaching your client that what you do, advertising, is very important to the success or failure of the client's business. The logic is clear. You can have the best product or service in the world and good salespeople. But your chances of becoming successful are slim to nil if your potential customers have no idea who you are, what you do, or how to get in touch with you. The best known corporations in the world understand that they must continue to advertise on a regular basis. But chances are that right now most independent businesses are concentrating a vast majority of their time, resources, and money on the other two sides of that triangle—sales force and product/service. What a shame. If so, our side, the short side that says advertising, is probably the side that needs more attention and in most cases, more budget than we're getting now.

The second reason to describe the marketing triangle to a client is to try to bring marketing problems to the surface. Often, marketing problems are not addressed by the media salesperson. And when the campaign fails, you and your station get the blame.

Implied Needs Questions.

WHAT DOES YOUR MARKETING TRIANGLE LOOK LIKE?

Here's another thing to ponder. As a broadcast salesperson, what does your marketing triangle look like? What percentage of the businesses in your signal coverage area even have a clue of **who** you are, **what** you do, and **how** to get in touch with you? How invisible are *you*?

W o r k s h e e t: Explaining Broadcast Marketing to a Direct Client

Advertising is one-third of the importance of the marketing success of a business. Ask your client, "What does your marketing triangle look like?"

1. As a broadcast account executive, what percentage of the businesses in your signal coverage area even have a clue of who you are, what you do, and how to get in touch with you? Draw your own marketing triangle. Be honest.

2. How do you routinely discuss marketing with your clients? If you don't usually discuss the topic, just jot down "I don't."

3. Brainstorm ways that you would approach your client if you suspected he or she had marketing problems.

CHAPTER

■■■ 5 ■■■

Advertising Clutter: You Are the Solution

L ots of business owners have their heads in the sand. Many are in a state of denial about how grave their situation has become, as they find themselves increasingly boxed in by big out-of-town box-stores. The idea in this chapter is to get your client paranoid enough that he begins to listen to you when you tell him that nowadays, he *must* advertise, or he'll be squashed like a house roach with a steel-toed boot.

There is no question that advertising clutter is getting worse, not better, for your client. It is essential that the client absolutely understands this. When she does, she'll be more open to ways you could help her survive, even against big national competitors.

HOMOGENIZATION DOESN'T JUST HAPPEN TO MILK

The world is becoming a much more homogenized place. We live in a changing and much more competitive business world, where a street in Austin, Texas, looks just like a street in Sacramento, California, which looks just like a street in Wichita, Kansas, that looks just like a street in Orlando, Florida, with box-stores and chains like Wal-Mart and Home Depot and T.J. Maxx and

McDonald's and Office Max and Lowe's and Applebee's and Wendy's and National Tire and Battery all lined up right next to each other.

These national chains are fiercely competing with each other and in the process they are eating smaller, family-owned businesses for lunch. Big businesses and smaller ones are competing for the same consumer dollars. It's literally a game of survival of the fittest. Both small town local businesses and major corporations are going out of business due to this new invasion of national, big box-stores. And it's not just retailers who are affected. Service-oriented businesses such as heating and a/c repair are also threatened by new national chains. Murders and executions—uh, sorry, I mean, mergers and acquisitions—continue their relentless homogenization of the world. The stakes are getting much higher. The game of doing business is getting tougher and tougher, whether you're a giant conglomeration or just a small family business.

Look around at many of our small-town, or even larger city business districts. Some look like ghost towns. Many old family stores are now closed. The doors and windows are being boarded up. And just a few miles away, the new homogenized box-store businesses appear to be doing quite well, all lined up with their bright, shiny signs, brand-new facades, and full parking lots.

LIVING IN THE SHADOW OF DARTH VADER

Nowadays, if your client isn't out there waving his arms and screaming, "Hey, don't forget about us! We're right here! HEY! WE'RE OVER HERE!" your client's huge competitors will finish him. He must promote his business in order to compete. If he doesn't devote more time and resources to expand the bottom line of his marketing triangle's bottom line, he'll get eaten alive. Scary, huh? Also true.

One could certainly argue that competing for consumer mindshare in this overcluttered, homogenized new century is a real dilemma. But is your client's situation hopeless? Or could it still be possible for her business to successfully compete for a greater share of consumer dollars? And, if she doesn't, what's the alternative? Should she just give up? Shut down? Crawl into a cave, curl up, and die? No, but she does have to advertise, and she needs to do it with frequency.

FREQUENCY OF THREE? BAH, HUMBUG

Back in the 1960s, a psychologist said that in order to break through advertising clutter, you would need to achieve a frequency of three with consumers. In other words, a consumer would have to see or hear an ad at least three times before making a decision on whether to buy. That was back in the 1960s.

Now here we are forty-some-odd years later. Should we still be recommending a frequency of three? I don't think so. Nowadays advertising is everywhere. Just open your eyes and ears and you'll realize that with increased advertising, sponsorships, and marketing clutter, perhaps more logically we should be recommending a frequency of at least six, maybe even eight.

Tell your clients that it is now believed that the average person, including your client, is exposed to a minimum of 5,000 commercial impressions every day. That estimate is up substantially from the early 1990s when researchers had estimated the number at a mere 2,500 per day. This jump is significant, and as you can imagine, global access to the Internet, high-speed connections, text messaging, spam, smart phones, more cable and satellite channels, increased media sponsorships, and the proliferation of magazines and websites have all played a role in this huge increase of media clutter. You might best explain this phenomenon by simply going through some of the commercial impressions made on you in the course of one day.

IN THE COURSE OF ONE DAY . . .

Just for one day, try to keep up with the companies that are trying to get your attention. I did it this morning and here are just some of the things I found.

I wake up in the morning and look at the word TIMEX on my alarm clock and then I hear commercials on my favorite radio station. I get out of bed and put on a bathrobe that says FLAMINGO HOTEL LAS VEGAS. I go downstairs and put RUTA MAYA coffee beans into a blender that says BRAUN. I then put the ground coffee in to a KRUPS coffee machine. I use BORDEN'S milk and IMPERIAL sugar. I pour SPECIAL K cereal into a bowl and chop up a CHIQUITA (not a media salesperson but a banana). I check my watch that says TAG-HEUER and go upstairs to turn on my favorite morning program on my PANASONIC television set. I take a shower and use NEUTROGENA shampoo and DOVE soap. I shave with a MACH-3 razor. I use an ORAL-B toothbrush and CREST toothpaste. Then I apply OLD SPICE antiperspirant and RALPH LAUREN cologne. Even my underwear is labeled with CALVIN KLEIN. Gosh, for what it costs it should say PAUL WEYLAND. My shirt says RALPH LAUREN. Shouldn't Ralph be paying US to wear those shirts? I take another sip of coffee from a mug with a TV CHANNEL 24 logo on it, and I just sit and wonder how many other commercial impressions I was actually exposed to but might have missed. I haven't even left the house yet. I haven't even checked my email. Unbelievable! For fun, just try for a day to keep up with the products and services that you are exposed to. It will amaze you. Write them down. *Memorize them.* Discuss them with your client. You'll find the client often jumps into the discussion, remembering products and services that he's exposed to in the course of a normal day. For many clients, this may be the first time they've ever actually looked at the big picture, at how much clutter there really is out there and what they're really up against. Why not point out what your local direct client is facing? A discussion like this really helps your client put things in perspective.

Once the client sees how vulnerable his "invisibility" makes him in this overcluttered world, he becomes more open to owning a day, a day-part, or a program on your station. A long-term contract on your station might start making absolute sense to the client.

SOMETHING ELSE TO MAKE YOU CRAZY

Here's another little thing to think about, just for you. Your proposal and presentation to a client is just one of 5,000 commercial impressions that your client is exposed to in the course of a normal day. Will your presentation to your client stand out, or just get lost in the clutter?

If your presentation identifies and solves a significant client problem, I guarantee you will stand out in that client's mind. Just imagine for a moment. If someone came along and identified and solved your biggest problem for you, how would you feel about that person? You'd feel gratitude. That person would be special, even indispensable to you. You might feel as though you owe that person something.

If you could learn to focus on identifying and solving problems for local direct broadcast clients, many of them would respect and admire you as well. If you, out of all of the client's vendors, media and otherwise, owned a position in the client's mind for solving her problems, you would stand out from the herd. You and your ideas might become topics of conversation that the client has outside of the workplace. Someone as valuable as you could benefit in many ways. Your phone calls would likely be taken immediately. You might always be a welcome visitor. Yes, you would certainly stand out from the thousands of others vying for your client's attention and budget.

W o r k s h e e t: Advertising Clutter: You Are the Solution

The purpose of this exercise is twofold: to help make you aware that the average person is exposed to a *minimum* of 5,000 commercial impressions per day, and your sales call is just *one* of 5,000 commercial impressions that your *client* is being exposed to in a single day.

1. Advertising clutter is getting worse, not better. Think about your normal daily routine and write a list of the products and services that you are exposed to in the course of a normal day. Make a copy of your list and start memorizing it so you can give your clients personal examples of how much advertising clutter each of us is inundated with in a single day.

2. Your client is being exposed to 5,000 commercial impressions a day, *including your sales call*. As a salesperson, describe two specific actions you will take in the next seven days to make your "1 in 5,000" impression stand out with your client.

   a. _____

   b. _____

CHAPTER
■■■ 6 ■■■

How We Really See and Hear Commercials

The information in this chapter on how we really see and hear advertising, combined with the concepts from the next chapter on branding, are very important to convey to local direct clients for the following three reasons:

1. To convince the client that his or her spot *can* be seen or heard, despite increased marketing clutter.
2. To begin the process of managing the client's expectations about results on your station.
3. To give the client more reasons for buying a long-term contract, regardless of whether your station is rated number one or number twenty.

WHY MANAGING CLIENT EXPECTATIONS ABOUT RESULTS IS SO IMPORTANT

The concept of how we really see and hear advertising will help you tell a compelling story to your clients about why they need to maintain a constant presence on your station. But there is another reason for teaching your clients how people really see and hear advertising: to start the process of managing the client's expectations about results on your station.

Nothing is worse for a broadcast account executive than getting a cancellation because the client thinks that his or her campaign on your station "isn't working." Many new broadcast clients naively perceive that a campaign on a station is worthless unless it results in huge crowds of people at their doorsteps. In subsequent chapters we will cover in detail the problem of managing client expectations about results. For right now, we begin that process of managing our client's expectations about results by explaining in a logical way why we don't have to reach everybody in order to have a good campaign.

EXPLAINING THE CONCEPT OF SELECTIVITY

Understanding that we're all inundated with a minimum of 5,000 commercial impressions per day, it's easy to see how we must filter out a majority of the information we're not interested in and only allow those things we're *on* for to filter in. This explains why we see and hear advertising selectively.

For example, let's look at how we really listen to the radio. In the United States, most people listen to the radio in their cars. Radio people will hate me for saying this, but it's true. We use the radio for environment and company. The radio may be on, but we're not really listening. Instead, we're concentrating on other things. Maybe we're thinking about the hot date we had last night. Or, we're worrying about the horrible day we're going to have today. Or, we're checking out the good-looking person in the car next to us. Or, we're looking at the not-so-good-looking person in the good-looking car next to us. Or, we're talking on a cell phone. Or, we're putting on makeup in the car. Or, we're having a conversation with a friend or relative in the car.

But even if we're having a conversation with a friend or relative in the car, what happens when your favorite song comes on the radio? What do you do? That's right, you turn up the volume. So, we listen to the radio selectively. Every single time I illustrate this to clients, they always make the motion of turning up a radio, or they say, "You turn it up." This clearly indicates that they are on the same page you're on.

BROKEN ENGINES AND LIGHT SWITCHES

People aren't really that difficult to figure out. We're like light switches. Either we are *on* or we're *off* for various products and services. We clearly see those products and services that we're interested in, and we filter out most of the rest of the clutter.

For example, I started noticing engine problems on my vehicle. The car was no longer under warranty. I took it in for repairs. Three weeks later I had a different problem. Again, I took it in to the shop. This problem was unrelated to the first. The two repairs cost well over $1,500. Within two months I had a third problem with the vehicle. Although I no longer had car payments, I began focusing on how much I was spending in repairs. I began to hate my car and started to rationalize replacing it.

One day I noticed a new sport SUV on display at a shopping mall. It looked very cool. I wondered what it would be like to test drive that car. The same day I noticed someone driving the same make and model. Clearly, I was now *on* for that vehicle. Then, on an international flight a week later, I saw a positive review of that vehicle in a British newspaper. Once I arrived in the UK, I "noted" a couple of versions of the same model and began pointing them out to my wife and friend. *On?* You bettcha.

Returning to the States, armed with the positive review in the British paper, I could hardly wait to test drive the vehicle. Was I *on?* I focused on radio and television commercials featuring that model. Soon I "happened by" the dealership. I test drove the car and the salesperson suggested I keep the car overnight. Friends and relatives actually congratulated me on my new purchase. At first I told them that it wasn't mine, I was just trying it out, but soon I realized that I was actually telling people the vehicle was mine. I was now not only *on* but *sold.*

For the first several weeks I owned the new car I saw my make and model everywhere. I still heard and saw advertisements about my car. But at this point I hardly ever notice them any more. Now, I'm *off*. All of those ads and spots have mysteriously disappeared.

ON AND OFF

Can you think of a particular product or service that you are *on* for right now? If you have a broken plumbing line, you're really *on* for a plumbing service. If you have a certain medical condition, you're *on* for any news or advertisement regarding that particular illness. If you are *on* for a new television, you'll pay more attention to any advertising you see or hear regarding a new set.

Recently, I was *on* for a new forty-two-inch plasma flat-screen television. I watched one at a friend's house. And from that moment on, I was hooked. Suddenly I saw flat-screened horizontal tvs everywhere. I noticed the arrival and departure screens at the airport. I watched every commercial I saw with a flat-screen tv. I paid very careful attention to every ad in the newspaper. If I got a piece of junk mail with a big plasma tv on it, that mailing was not junk to me. Now that I've had one for a while, I generally don't see those ads or spots any more.

WHY WE DON'T HAVE TO REACH EVERYBODY

When you're advertising, you don't have to reach everybody. In fact, reaching everybody would be physically and theoretically impossible. And, it's very unrealistic to think that you could reach everybody. To do so, you'd have to run commercials and ads in every single medium, on every station and publication. And, you'd have to run those spots every minute of every hour, every day. Then of course, when people tuned into a station, all they would see or hear is your ad, and they'd turn off their sets. You'd have to have full-page ads in every single publication. No editorial, just ads. And then of course, nobody would buy the publication. So, you can't reach everybody and you don't have to.

Visualize your station as a lake filled with fish. I know that some people hate comparing customers to fish, but the example works. In each lake, including yours, there are fish that are hungry for what your client is selling right now. If you cast good bait and cast that bait often enough, provided that you don't have marketing problems (and provided that particular lake is not being overfished by your client's competitors), it looks like a pretty good calculated risk that your client could catch fish. *Providing your target & the client's target match.*

EXPLAINING SELECTIVE VIEWING AND LISTENING TO LOCAL DIRECT CLIENTS

Here again, is the way you would explain this concept to your clients.

Radio

Most people are listening in their cars. Others listen through headphones, at work or at home. Usually, they only listen for ten to twenty minutes at a time, but with today's bad traffic, people are listening for longer periods of time. Okay, let's admit it to the client. People turn on the radio for environment and companionship. They are *hearing* the radio but they're not really *listening* to every word and every song on that station. Instead, they are concentrating on the task of driving or thinking about their day or talking on a mobile phone or having a conversation.

For example, if you're in the market for a new green Toyota convertible and you're thinking about buying one in the near future, you would be highly likely to listen to a radio commercial that began, "Green Toyota convertibles are the most beautiful cars on the road." Or if you're refinancing your house, you're likely to listen to every single mortgage commercial and ad talking about refinancing. If you've just had a fender-bender, you're much more likely to listen to commercials about auto body repair. If you're getting engaged soon, it's very likely that you'll listen to commercials about engagement rings and wedding sets. See what I mean? We listen to radio commercials selectively.

Television

It's the same situation as radio. The longer people stay in their homes, the more likely it is that they'll spend more time watching television and seeing more television commercials. But again, let's admit something to the client that he or she will be able to relate to. People *see* many television commercials but they actually *watch* very few of them. People watch commercials about subjects they are really interested in.

In other words, if you're in the market for a product or service that you will buy this week from somebody, you will immediately take careful notice if a spot targets you with that particular product or service. If you've been injured on the job, you're much more likely to see commercials from personal injury attorneys. If you're in the market for a new bedroom set, you're highly likely to notice commercials from furniture stores. So we also watch television commercials selectively.

We don't have to reach everybody with an advertising campaign on our station, just a percentage of those people who are *on*. There are many viewers or listeners out there who are not *on* for what the client is selling right now. But they might be *on* next week, or next month, or in three months.

Provided that the client doesn't have marketing problems or that his or her business is seasonal, and provided your station is reaching the proper demographic, then it is logical that there are fish *on* for your client's product or service constantly. That's why the client must fish on your lake constantly throughout the year. Every time he's not casting, he's missing hungry fish. And for fish who aren't hungry for his product or service right now, he's going to get them used to seeing and hearing his bait by branding them. In the next chapter we'll discuss branding.

W o r k s h e e t: How We Really See and Hear Commercials

Identify a couple of clients in a product/service category not "over-fished" on your "lake." Put a pitch together incorporating the idea that the client does not have to reach everyone in order to have a successful campaign, just a percentage of people who are "on."

———→ *Unless you have gang-buster creative!*

CHAPTER

■■■ 7 ■■■

Branding—It's Not Just for Cowboys

WHAT IS BRANDING?

Let me let you in on a little secret. Remember that old media buzz word "branding"? Well, here's how branding relates to you and how it can help you sell a lot more long-term broadcast advertising schedules. Tell your client that it is in his or her best interest to launch a long-term branding campaign on your station. With repeated reminders, listeners or viewers will begin associating your client with that particular product or service.

Many local businesses are slowly losing market share to bigger competitors. And if they're losing market share, that also means they're losing mind share. What is mind share? It's the portion of the consumer's mind that is owned by a particular brand. If a company owns enough mind share in enough people, it probably also takes in a significant share of market revenue in that product or service category. Market share means mind share. Mind share means market share.

Keep in mind that somebody lost a pair of glasses yesterday. Somebody else is losing her glasses today, and more people will lose their glasses in coming days, weeks, or months. The people who have lost their glasses are *on* for eyewear. But instead of leaving things totally up to chance, the client should start branding your audience so that when listeners or viewers finally come *on*, instead of just thinking about one or two vendors when it's time to buy, perhaps they'll think of your client's product or service as well.

Here is how an optician could brand your audience.

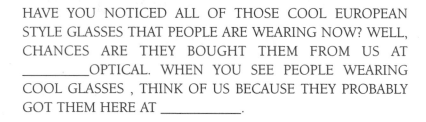

HAVE YOU NOTICED ALL OF THOSE COOL EUROPEAN STYLE GLASSES THAT PEOPLE ARE WEARING NOW? WELL, CHANCES ARE THEY BOUGHT THEM FROM US AT _____OPTICAL. WHEN YOU SEE PEOPLE WEARING COOL GLASSES , THINK OF US BECAUSE THEY PROBABLY GOT THEM HERE AT _____.

Branding is a simple concept, and it means precisely what it says. When you brand livestock, you are leaving a permanent symbol that identifies that animal as a member of a specific herd. In the application of marketing, you are hoping to "brand" a client's particular product or service into the minds of consumers.

Branding establishes mind share. Consider this: When you think about the words "safe automobile," what brand comes to mind? Most people immediately say, "Volvo." It's no wonder. Volvo has spent millions and millions of dollars "etching" its identity with safe vehicles into our heads. Volvo has tattooed that idea into your head and it will never, never come out. When we're all in the nursing home, sucking on Ensure and sitting on Depends, someone will say, "Safe automobile." And we'll all jump up and say, "Volvo, Volvo, Volvo."

If I said the words, "great place to take the kids to get a hamburger," what brand immediately pops into your head? Of course you'd say, "McDonald's." When I asked this question at a seminar recently, a Burger King executive just shook his head in frustration and sighed when everyone else in the room shouted, "McDonald's!"

Had I said, "Expensive watch," most people would immediately say, "Rolex."

How about "lumber and hardware"? Does Home Depot or Lowe's come to mind? This kind of big box-store mind share is killing smaller, locally owned hardware stores.

These major companies have spent a great deal of time and money trying to "brand" their products and services into the tissues of our minds. Some businesses have done a great job with branding. Many, many more are failing miserably.

Branding works on a local level as well, and if your client's business isn't somehow branding her products and services into the minds of potential consumers (your audience, for example), she is in danger of losing those potential consumers to competitors who are branding successfully. Suggest to your client that she ask people who are not friends or customers who they think about when she mentions her business's product or service specialty. Will they mention the name of your client's business? Or is it possible that she's invisible to most of the very people she needs to be reaching?

Draw a circle on a piece of paper and put little Xs inside the circle. This image represents a bird's eye view of the top of the head of a listener or viewer—in other words, a potential customer. The Xs represent the products and services that this individual knows and trusts, because those product companies have made an investment in branding him or her. Now draw a little X outside of the circle. This X represents your client's company, if he's not successfully reaching out and branding that person with the image of his company. Consider that right now, provided your client doesn't have marketing problems, there are customers right this minute who would like to be doing business with him, but to most potential customers, he is completely invisible. Or even worse, his company might have a negative branding problem.

NEGATIVE BRANDING?

Branding works both ways, both positive and negative. Is it possible that even if people manage to think about your client's business at all, they're thinking that he's too expensive or that he has a poor selection? What if your client is branded with, "not open or available when I need to shop"? Are people thinking that his business is difficult to find? How about bad service or no place to park? What if they're thinking that he has a grungy-looking building? Or, surly-looking or acting employees?

Is it possible that your client's business has a negative branding problem that she doesn't even notice? You know that old saying, "She can't see the forest for the trees." Sometimes business owners are so wrapped up in their own little worlds that they lose sight of what others might clearly perceive.

Have you ever had a piece of gravel hit the windshield of your car? At first, you see a pockmark in the glass. Then, a small crack appears. And then the crack gets a little bigger. If you don't act and fix the glass quickly, the crack starts to disappear. It's still there, but you just don't see it any more. The crack becomes completely invisible to you. Is it possible that your client's business has a negative branding "crack" that he can't see? How are potential customers branding his business? What might they see that your client is not seeing?

People seldom comment to others about routine experiences with businesses. But they always seem to remember their bad experiences. And then they relate those bad experiences to other people. Most of us have had a bad experience with some type of business. I know of a restaurant in my city that has a beautiful view of the lake. People go there to drink and watch the colorful sunsets, but they definitely do not go there for the food. Years ago, that restaurant was "branded" with having bad food. The word spread quickly. "We go there for a margarita and for the sunset on the lake, but don't order the food there; it's terrible."

The restaurant owners didn't get it. They continued to waste money on advertising because of their marketing problem, trying to convince people that the food there was really good. It didn't work. They were already negatively branded. At one point, they just gave up, shut down the kitchen, and told people to bring their own food when they came to drink and watch the sunset. One day, many years later, the restaurant burned down. The newspaper article on the fire even mentioned that the restaurant was never known for its food.

Sometimes, it's no wonder that people in your community can't wait for the big, homogenized box-store to open in their neighborhood. Over time, they've developed the perception that the local company they'd been doing business with was "ripping them off" with high prices, poor selection, no parking, bad service, and a grungy, uninviting storefront. So, when the shiny new place opens, they rush to it like moths to a flame. People are creatures of habit. We tend to shop the same stores and frequent the same restaurants and bars, that is, until we've just had it, or when something newer and better comes along. Why would your client give them any reason to change their habits and shop at the newer, shinier competitor?

We've been shopping at the same neighborhood grocery store for years. It's convenient to our home. Some time back, the store initiated a "loyalty card" system. With the implementation of that system, we perceived that prices seem much higher at our store than at other grocery stores. The selection and the service appear to be getting worse. Still we shopped there, strictly out of habit and convenience.

Then one day I went in to pick up a few things. I spent about $78. The checker asked me for my card. I told her I didn't have it. I'd left it at home or my wife had it. "Too bad," she said. "You would have saved $6.53." I asked her to use her card so I could get the discount I'd earned. "Sorry," she said. "We're not allowed to use our cards any more when the customer forgets his. If you don't have the card, then you lose the discount." "Then get the manager," I demanded (the people with carts behind me rolled their eyes and muttered curse words).

When the manager heard the story he said, "Too bad, sir. If you had your card you would have saved $6.53." "Oh, I'll get my discount," I insisted. "Use your card." "We can't do that for you, sir. But if you'll kindly go to the Customer Service Area and fill out a short form, we'll get you another card," he told me. "I'd rather peel out my corneas with my thumbnails than stand in line to fill out another one of your forms," I said. "Look up my phone number in your computer. You'll see every steak, head of lettuce, every box of cereal, and every tampon we've ever bought in this store. We spend about $200 a week in this store. Over fifteen years, that makes us close to a $150,000 customer. And if I don't get my $6.53 RIGHT NOW, I'M MARCHING MY $150,000 BUTT OUT OF THIS STORE AND I'M NEVER COMING BACK!" "Here's your $6.53." he said meekly. Other customers started applauding, and not just because I was finished holding up the line. Several people told me they too were sick of the "loyalty card."

A new chain grocery store is opening soon, about three minutes further away. We can't wait. Instead of victimizing customers with the card, they discount the merchandise right off the shelves. We've had it with our old store and soon they'll lose a $150,000 loyal customer.

Remember what we said? Advertising a business with marketing problems is like putting lipstick on a pig. Provided your client doesn't have marketing problems, he must somehow advertise and begin a positive branding process, or he risks being totally invisible to potential customers.

"WORD OF MOUTH IS THE BEST KIND OF ADVERTISING"

Have you heard the objection, "Word of mouth is the best kind of advertising"? When I hear that I immediately say, "Yes, you're absolutely right. Word of mouth is the best kind of advertising. But it could also be the worst. One bad experience for a customer could destroy a fifty-year reputation for your client. One rude employee could blow a good reputation for your client. If you have a good experience at a restaurant, you might tell a few people. But what if you have a bad restaurant experience? Who are you going to tell? You're going to tell *everybody*.

"Radio and television advertising is controlled word of mouth. You control the words. One reason for maintaining a long-term advertising campaign with our station is to provide a layer of positive, controlled word of mouth to consumers to help put out little fires of insurgence that pop up when a customer has a negative experience with your company, Mr. Client." Tell your client that consistent, controlled word of mouth advertising is an excellent insurance policy against bad word of mouth advertising from dissatisfied customers or from your client's competitors.

Is branding important to your client? The answer is absolutely. Good, positive mind share means everything when trying to increase your market share. Now your client has three excellent reasons to buy your station long-term:

1. To reach a percentage of those people who are *on* for his product or service right now.

2. For everybody else, he's starting the branding process for those people who are not *on* right now, but might be on later.

3. As insurance against bad word of mouth.

W o r k s h e e t: Branding: It's Not Just for Cowboys

1. Briefly describe how you would explain the importance of broadcast advertising in establishing your client's brand.

2. Explain how advertising with you could help your client to dispel "bad word of mouth" advertising.

CHAPTER
▪▪▪ 8 ▪▪▪

Your Station Is the
Logical Solution

So far we have covered five concepts in our study of how to get the client on the same page we're on regarding the logic of marketing and advertising. This chapter covers the sixth and final marketing concept, the pure logic of using your station. Subsequent chapters will cover the difference between good and bad advertising and how to calculate ROI (return on investment).

FIVE MARKETING CONCEPTS PREVIOUSLY COVERED

- **Easy.** What we do for a living is not difficult; it's easy and it makes logical sense. Any business will benefit from more people knowing who it is, what it does, and how to get in touch with it. We represent thousands of pairs of eyes and ears with legs and wallets.

- **Marketing Triangle.** Although what we do is just as important as the client's product or service and his or her sales force, advertising is usually the weakest side in the client's marketing triangle.

- **5,000.** We know now that the average person is exposed to a minimum of 5,000 commercial impressions per day. Marketing clutter is getting worse every year, not better. Nowadays, businesses must advertise or they're invisible.

- **Branding.** With all of the clutter out there, businesses must brand their products or services into the minds of consumers. How difficult is a client making it for your audience to do business with him if they don't know who he is, what he does, or how to get in touch with him?

- **How we really see and hear advertising.** Consumers see and hear many commercials. However, they watch and listen selectively based on products and services that they are interested in purchasing right now. We're trying to effectively reach those people who are *on* for particular products and services and will buy them this week. For everybody else, we are beginning the branding process.

Now here's a very important sixth and final step in the marketing education process. Stress the logic of advertising on your station. Let the client know that using your station is not a crapshoot, but instead a good, calculated risk. This step is easy to understand and is vital information for you to give your client to think about. This step does the following three things:

1. Help convince a local direct client that your station is a logical buy, regardless of your audience ranking.

2. Continue the process of managing the client's expectations about advertising results on your station. Remember that you don't have to reach everybody, just those people who are *on* for your client's product or service right now.

3. Get the client to begin thinking more about whether she's getting her fair share of the total market for her product or service.

IT'S REALLY LOGICAL TO ADVERTISE WITH US

I use the words, "Look, it's logical," or "Do you see the logic here?" often during my presentations with clients. And guess what? They always nod their heads affirmatively when I say those words. The reason? The word logical means reasonable and responsible. And, we all want to do the responsible, reasonable thing.

Here's some real logic for your client to ponder. Provided the client does not have marketing problems, it is logical and statistically likely that a percentage of any populated area will buy the client's product or service from somebody this week. If your format or your program fits demographically with your client's product or service, it is also logical and statistically likely that a similar percentage of your station's audience will also be buying what your client is selling from somebody this week. However, how can your audience buy from your client if she's not advertising to them? Again, how difficult is your client making it for the people who watch or listen to your station to do business with her and her company?

At this point, ask your client if she knows how many people in your market will buy her product or service from either her or her competitors this month. If she doesn't know the answer to that, perhaps you could help her by offering to contact one of her suppliers or a professional association for the correct information. With this data, your client will be better able to estimate her share of total revenues in her product or service category. If she's not the industry leader, she will begin to understand that she has a lot of work to do on the bottom line of her marketing triangle. You and the audience of consumers you represent are there to help her expand her bottom line.

Some clients have been trained to believe that your station has no value unless you're number one. Clearly, this is just another misconception born of ignorance. Every audience is valuable. Whether you're number one is not a valid issue. Here's a great way to deflect your client's misconception. "You know, Mr. Client, you're not number one in your industry, either. And I don't have to be number one in mine. I still represent thousands of consumers who will buy your product/service from somebody this week. How difficult are you making it for them to buy from you when you don't teach them who you are, what you do, and how to get in touch with you? Furthermore, different people listen to different stations. By advertising only with one station you're missing potential customers that watch or listen here. Also keep in mind that because we're not 'number one,' fewer of your competitors are advertising with us. Here you're a bigger fish.

"Mr. Client, provided my audience matches your desired customer and you don't have marketing problems, then it is also logical and statistical that a nice percentage of the people watching my television station or listening to my radio station will also buy your product or service from you *or* your competitor this week. How difficult are you making it for that segment of our thousands of viewers or listeners to do business with you and your company if they don't know who you are, what you do, or how to get in touch with you?"

This kind of thinking makes a powerful case for your client to sign a long-term contract and always maintain a presence on your station. Remember, that provided the client does not have marketing problems and provided you're demographically in sync with your client, in any given week, logically and statistically, members of your audience will be *on*. That is, in the market for what your client is selling. But how can they buy from your client if he's not constantly reminding them of who he is, what he does and how to get in touch with him?

Tell the client there is no money wasted on your station. We cast good bait into a lake filled with hungry fish often enough and we'll catch fish. If you're not fishing consistently on this lake then, logically, you're missing customers. And logically, a good number of those fish who aren't hungry now will be hungry for what you're selling sooner or later. By getting them used to the bait we're casting on a regular basis, we're *branding* them.

Now we have three good reasons your client should invest in a long-term presence on your station, regardless of your ratings, format, or program.

1. To catch fish that are logically and statistically his. Unless your client's business is seasonal, there are listeners or viewers coming to the surface of your lake each and every week

looking to buy what your client is selling. Each week your client doesn't fish in your lake, he's missing sales.

2. For those who aren't ready to buy this week, he's starting the branding process.

3. Insurance against bad word of mouth.

And here is a fourth reason it's in your client's best interest to have a long-term relationship with you and your station. It's an emotional reason but it's a good one.

We are the client's "ticket to the show." When your client signs a long-term agreement with you, imply that in addition to all of the logical reasons he has for doing so, he gets preferred client status. That means several good things. For example, he may get rate advantages. His spots are booked in advance and are less likely to get bumped. But here's another larger reason it's in his best interest to have a long-term relationship with you. You become the client's conduit to the entertainment world. Face it, we're in the entertainment business. What we do for a living is generally perceived to be cool and exciting. Most local direct clients have never been to a radio or television station before. We're more fun to work with than the client's other vendors. Let's take advantage of that. Now with the long-term contract, he's going to get to visit often. He becomes friends with on-air personalities and management. You may be able to supply him and his family with CDs, DVDs, video games, concert tickets, theater openings, films, travel, and other special perks. He achieves a certain social status with friends and relatives who do not have his influence in the entertainment world. Through special events hosted by your station, he meets other "movers and shakers" who own businesses in your community. Ladies and gentlemen, we are in show business. The problem nowadays is that too much of the show is gone and it's become just plain business. Let's put the show back in show business and share the fun with our clients. We could change the client's social and professional life by introducing him to new business contacts. He could get new accounts. His relationship with you could provide him, his family, his friends and business associates with the best tickets in town. As long as he pays, he plays.

W o r k s h e e t: Your Station Is the Logical Solution

1. Use the information you learned from this chapter to create a pitch for a prospect. Customize the six marketing concepts we've discussed for that customer.

2. Assuming that your demographic is appropriate and your client doesn't have marketing problems, why is it logical for a local direct client to buy a long-term contract on your station, whether you're number one or not?

PART

II

Writing Genius Creative Whether You're a Creative Genius or Not

CHAPTER
■■■ 9 ■■■

Recognizing Creative Problems

Over the next five chapters, we will discuss the differences between good and bad advertising and how you can help your client gain a competitive edge by using more effective creative messages. If you know what you're doing and the local direct client knows you know what you're doing, you will "drive the bus" when it comes to the creative part of the business. Instead of the client telling you what to do, you'll be in control, with an iron-clad and logical creative plan. You may become the client's expert when it comes to creative expertise. Consequently, the client will begin looking at you as though you are an expert rather than just another pest. This gives you power and influence. The creative process will go much more smoothly. The client will rely on your creative expertise, and you will save valuable time rewriting copy.

Think about it this way. If you went to the doctor and he told you to "take two of these pills each day," it is unlikely that you would say, "No! I'm going to take four." And, if you had legal or tax problems, you would listen very carefully to your attorney or your accountant. We pay these professionals very well, because we perceive them as being experts in a particular field and a valuable asset. However, in our business the client, again usually uneducated, tells us what should or should not go into a spot. Consequently, our commercials wind up looking and sounding like, well, commercials. There is no headline to grab attention immediately. They are riddled with clichés. The call-to-action may be vague or hidden. And when the campaign "doesn't work," who will the client blame? You and your station.

With the average person exposed to a minimum of 5,000 commercial impressions per day, *if advertising isn't outstanding, it won't stand out at all.*

A good spot always contains four important elements (which we'll cover in detail in the following chapters):

1. An identifiable difference
2. An emotional headline
3. Benefits and results without clichés
4. A crystal-clear call-to-action

THE CREATIVE PROBLEM

You can bet that 90 percent of the time, horrible creative had a huge role to play in the advertising campaign that "didn't work." That is, the script is so poorly written that the commercial has little or no effect in selling the viewer or listener on the client's product or service. This is a huge problem that can be easily corrected, regardless of whether you think of yourself as a creative genius.

At a NAB Europe event, I met a Russian promotions director named Anna. Anna had attended my creative workshop in Lisbon. She said, "You are so correct about the horrible creative situation. We have a big automotive client in Moscow. His commercial was driving away our listeners. He was running a song by Pink Floyd (an ASCAP/BMI violation), but he has changed the lyrics to his own stupid song. Listeners were calling us and telling us that he was wrecking their lives by screwing up one of their favorite songs and that they would no longer be listening to our station."

Anna went to her sales director and told her that the commercial had to be changed. The director told Anna that the client had paid cash in advance for a year and that she was not going to call and bother the client, but that it was okay if Anna called. So Anna did. She met with the automotive dealer and here is her version of the conversation.

Anna: "Think of your commercial as the front of your building. You want it to be inviting to people who come in. But your commercial is horrible, and it makes you look bad."

Client: "I like my commercial. Listeners like it."

Anna: "No, they don't. They hate it. Think of it like this. What if I took a photo of a big, fat, hairy man butt and blew it up real big and pasted it on the front of your building? That is how your commercial makes you look."

Client: "You can't compare my commercial to a big, fat, hairy man butt."

Anna: "Yes, I can. Instead of making you look good, your commercial makes you look like an ass."

This was a harsh way of telling the client that his creative was hurting him more than it was helping him. You might consider using a more subtle approach, but the bottom line is that, finally, the client understood what Anna was saying and he changed his commercial. How many "big, fat, hairy man butt" spots are running on your station? Most of them make the client look bad, and they are not effective in luring listeners or viewers to the client's businesses.

These next few chapters deal with the subject of creative. By the time you finish these chapters, you'll be an expert on the difference between good and bad advertising, regardless of whether you think you're a creative genius.

The other benefit you'll get from these upcoming chapters is a great new way to get appointments. By the time you're finished with this creative series, you will be able to say something like this to a client: "I saw/heard your ad/spot (on another station or in the paper or in the Yellow Pages). There's nothing wrong with that station (or other media), but in twenty minutes I could show you a way that you could increase the effectiveness and the efficiency of the advertising you're doing by 80 percent, whether you use my station or not." If someone came to me with a claim like that, I think I'd give her twenty minutes. But first, let's look at the creative problem.

WHY ADVERTISING DOESN'T WORK

Americans alone will spend over $230 billion on advertising in all media this year, and 80 to 90 percent of this money will be completely wasted. A majority of that waste is the result of poor copy. Bad bait. When a client says that he "tried radio or TV once and it didn't work," one or two or three or four or ALL FIVE of the following things had to go wrong:

1. Wrong demographic
2. Stingy schedule
3. Marketing problems
4. Mismanaged expectations about results
5. Horrible, horrible creative

Creative problems and mismanaged expectations about results are the two biggest problems. Unfortunately, most broadcast creative is just horrible. Instead of producing copy that would modify the behavior of listeners and viewers and drive them to our clients, we produce cliché-infested, wallpaper garbage that has little chance of breaking through the 5,000 commercial impressions that the average listener or viewer is exposed to in a single day.

THE BLANK SHEET OF PAPER TEST

If you were trying to sell a piece of white paper, would it make logical sense to hold that paper up against a white background, or a dark background? The obvious answer is the dark background.

Why? Because the white paper would stand out against the dark background. Holding that sheet of white paper against a white background would be camouflage, like wallpaper.

The same principle applies to advertising. The last thing we want are spots that look like or sound like spots. That would be camouflage. And nowadays with the 5,000 commercial impressions per day that we're all exposed to, camouflage would mean sabotage. The last thing any of us would want to do is sabotage a client's advertising message, but we do it all of the time.

The reason is that we in media sales and the clients we're working with all believe that a radio or tv commercial is supposed to sound like or look like a commercial. This is why, when it's time to talk advertising creative, that we begin using a foreign language, a foreign tongue that we only speak when we're talking advertising. I call that foreign language "ad-speak." Ad-speak is a language made up entirely of advertising clichés like, "But hurry, with prices like these, selection won't last long," or, "It's a holiday tradition," or, "Plenty of loyal and eager salespeople to assist you," or, "We're family owned and operated." In radio and television advertising, we have thirty or sixty seconds to create the ultimate seduction to a percentage of our listeners or viewers. Every single word must count. We have no room for clichés, and we certainly cannot afford to sabotage a client's advertising message in the commercials that we produce.

Think about this: The commercials that we air on our station are our product. Creative is such an important part of what we do that there is absolutely no room for winging it, but typically the broadcast account executive knows no more than the average client about the difference between good and bad advertising. Consequently, the tail winds up wagging the dog. The client, who is completely uneducated about the difference between good and bad advertising, shoots in the dark and tells the account executive what should or should not be in the spot. The account executive dutifully writes down everything the clients tells him to, and then delivers it to the production department. The production people may realize that the copy points are weak, but they're so busy that they overlook those weaknesses and quickly crank out another crappy spot. By default, the production department becomes a crap factory.

My production director friend, Jim Kipping, likens production directors to air traffic controllers. They may have only two runways (production facilities), but they always have eight aircraft (salespeople) trying to land. There is very little time for production people to come up with creative masterpieces for every one of your clients, especially when the copy points you've given them to work with are total rubbish.

Just because we got into this business by mistake is no reason to do business by mistake. If you are an account executive for a broadcast station, you *must* be knowledgeable about the creative process. There is no room for winging it when it comes to such an important part of the media sales process.

You don't have to be a creative genius to know the difference between good and bad advertising. You just need to understand the rules. If you know the rules of a game, it's much more likely that you have a chance of winning. When it comes to spot creative, most broadcast salespeople just don't know the rules. This creates many problems, including your client's (mismanaged) expectations about advertising results on your station.

By being on top of the creative process, you look more like a resource in the eyes of the client. Once the client understands that you know more about the creative process than he does, he'll surrender the keys, and you'll be driving the bus. Your superior creative skills will help make you stand out against the "human spam" of his other media representatives. The best commercials identify and solve consumer problems in language the consumer can easily understand and relate to.

W o r k s h e e t: Recognizing Creative Problems

1. Analyze your last few spots to make sure they don't suffer from any of the five reasons that advertising "doesn't work."

2. How can you make them pop more?

3. Write down two examples of cliché "ad-speak" expressions that you hear and see all of the time in commercials.

CHAPTER

■■■ 10 ■■■

Creating a Centerpiece
for Your Commercial

The first creative rule is the *unique selling proposition (USP)*, or *identifiable difference (ID)*. This is the kernel, the centerpiece, the skeleton, or the foundation on which you will build the rest of the spot.

The first thing you must do to create a great spot for a client is to help the client establish a unique selling proposition or identifiable difference. These two terms mean exactly the same thing. What is it about your client's business that makes her stand out from her competition? Clichés like "best service in town" don't mean anything to potential customers who are *on*. The identifiable difference you're looking for must be meaningful to the viewer or listener.

For example, if your client owns a restaurant, maybe he has one particular dish that he does better than any other restaurant in town. If the client is a dry cleaner, maybe he can get your clothes back to you in one hour or less. If it's a jeweler, perhaps the USP could be that she carries an exclusive, sought-after brand. If the client is a plumber, maybe he guarantees that he could provide service within one hour of your call.

The unique selling proposition should always be something that distinguishes your client from the rest of his competitors. It must be *meaningful* to those persons (people who are *on*) who will buy your client's product or service from somebody this week. It should never be clichéd.

USE THE "SO WHAT? WHAT'S IN IT FOR ME?" TEST

If the client has a slogan, look at it critically. If the slogan is clichéd and says something like "Best service in town," ask yourself, from the perspective of a potential buyer of your client's product or service, "So what? What's in it for ME?" *Best service* is camouflaged ad-speak. Push your client to find out what *best service* really means to a potential buyer.

I had a client who owned an auto body repair shop. When I spoke with him about spot content I asked him the question, "What makes your business different than your competition?" He immediately told me,"We offer the best service in town." I said, "But what does 'best service' really mean to me if I just wrecked my car?" The client said, "Well, all of our people are A.S.E. certified" (or something like that). I kept asking, "Yeah, but what's in it for me to come all the way over here and do business with you?" Finally, he said, "Well, if you come here, we'll loan you one of our cars until we get yours fixed." *Bingo*! There's an identifiable difference.

If you crash your car and you're not injured, what is your biggest problem? You don't have any transportation. It's a pain trying to go about the course of your normal day. You can't pick up the kids from school. You can't run your errands. You have to make a special effort to get transportation. This was his USP.

CHERCHEZ LE CRENEAU . . . LOOK FOR THE HOLE

The French say, "cherchez le creneau," which means "look for the hole." Help your advertiser find a "hole" that his competitors are not filling, and then fill that hole. Other body shops also offered to loan cars to customers while theirs were being fixed. The hole in this case was that nobody else was advertising it. So we agreed to own that position of loaning vehicles to customers while their cars were being fixed. The spot centered on that identifiable difference. It went something like this:

> IF YOU WRECK YOUR CAR AND YOU BRING IT TO US, WE'LL LOAN YOU ONE OF OUR CARS UNTIL YOUR CAR IS FIXED. AND WE'LL REPAIR YOUR VEHICLE QUICKLY AND COR-RECTLY, BECAUSE WE WANT OUR CAR BACK.

And, what if your client doesn't have a USP? Whose job would it be to help him discover one? That would be *your* job.

We had another client who owned a jewelry store. This client had no particular USP. He wanted to sell wedding sets and engage-ment rings. We came up with something that broke through the crap-o-sphere of all the other jewelry store advertisements that all looked and sounded the same. The client loved our idea and it worked for him. Here was his USP: "We can double the size of the diamond for about the same price you'd pay elsewhere for the smaller stone."

The spot focused on that USP and looked something like this.

> IF SHE SAYS SIZE DOESN'T MATTER, SHE'S LYING WHEN IT COMES TO DIAMONDS. AT " " JEWELERS, WE CAN DOUBLE THE SIZE OF THE DIAMOND FOR ABOUT THE SAME PRICE YOU'D PAY FOR THE SMALLER STONE. HOW? AT " " JEWEL-ERS, WE LOOK FOR GOOD DIAMONDS IN LARGER SIZES. THESE STONES ARE NOT ULTRA-PERFECT. THEY MIGHT CONTAIN AN INCLUSION NOT NORMALLY VISIBLE TO THE NAKED EYE. WHY NOT? WHEN WAS THE LAST TIME ANYBODY EVER ADMIRED YOUR DIAMOND WITH A MICRO-SCOPE? NEVER. " " DIAMONDS ARE REAL DIAMONDS. REALLY BIG DIAMONDS. THEY'RE WHITE AND THEY REALLY, REALLY SPARKLE. SO, INSTEAD OF A QUARTER-CARAT DIA-MOND, YOU COULD GET HER A HALF-CARAT. INSTEAD OF A HALF-CARAT, GET HER A FULL CARAT. FOR ABOUT THE SAME PRICE AS THE SMALLER STONE. THINK OF " " JEWELERS AS DIAMONDS ON STEROIDS. TELL HIM THAT

SIZE REALLY DOES MATTER . . . WHEN IT COMES TO DIA-
MONDS. GET HER A DIAMOND TWICE THE SIZE FOR
ABOUT THE SAME PRICE AT " " JEWELERS . . . DIAMONDS
ON STEROIDS . . . " " JEWELERS . . . (ADDRESS).

Guess what, it worked. We made it much easier for people who
were *on* for wedding and engagement rings to hear this spot. Our
commercial stuck out through the crap-o-sphere of all of those
other jewelry store commercials.

Guarantees and offers that minimize inconvenience are examples of a potentially strong USPs. For example, if your client is a
plumber, a great USP might be that if someone is not at your house
within twenty minutes, the service is free. As a consumer with a
nasty plumbing problem, you don't want to have to wait hours for
a plumber. This plumber's USP identifies and solves the customer's
problem in language the consumer can absolutely relate to.

Cliché IDs would include meaningless and obscure ad-speak
claims like, "friendly, knowledgeable employees," or "family-owned
and operated since 1997," or "for all of your insurance needs."
Other cliché ad-speak slogans include, "Our motto is to serve you,"
"Service second to none," and "You can count on us for the friendliest deal in town."

While we're on the subject, here's a good question. As a media
salesperson, what is *your* identifiable difference? What sets you
apart from the other media salespeople in your market? Do *you*
stand out from the clutter of all of the other media and vendor reps
that regularly visit your client? Or are you just another piece of
human spam?

W o r k s h e e t: Creating a Centerpiece for Your Commercial

The unique selling position should always be something that distinguishes your client from any competitors.

1. List a few current client or potential clients. Write down any Unique Selling Propositions these clients might have but aren't currently using. Remember, no clichés.

   Client _____ USP _____

   Client _____ USP _____

   Client _____ USP _____

   Client _____ USP _____

   Client _____ USP _____

2. What differentiating trait or identifiable difference would you like to have as a media salesperson?

CHAPTER

11

Making the Spot Emotional

The second creative rule is to get the target market's attention immediately. Remember, we're not trying to reach everybody. We don't have to do that. All we have to do is get the immediate attention of those viewers or listeners who are *on* for your client's product or service and will make a buying decision this week.

USE A HEADLINE

You notice that I say we should begin every spot with a headline. Why a headline? Well, think about why newspapers use headlines. They use them to get your attention, right? We should also use headlines at the beginning of our spots if we want to get the attention of the viewer or listener who will buy what your client is selling from somebody this week. For everyone else, we're starting the branding process. So, our spot must stand out enough to break through the clutter for listeners and viewers who are not *on* right now, but might be soon.

MAKE IT AN EMOTIONAL HEADLINE

Virtually all people share common emotions. Most of us can relate to envy, fear, shame, gratitude, and a host of other emotional feelings. Although we like to think that we buy logically, we really buy emotionally. In broadcast script writing many of us have forgotten the power of an emotional appeal. Instead, we bang away at the listener or viewer with hard, cold facts or empty promises. People relate and respond emotionally so why not use that power to help clients reach deeply into the hearts and minds of listeners and viewers? We then back up our emotional appeal with facts. It works and I can prove it. Here's what I mean.

Let's say I was trying to sell you a burglar alarm system for your home. I could try to appeal to your brain by giving you facts and figures about the alarm system like this:

WITH OUR NEW X-27 DIGITAL PROCESSOR WE'RE RUN-NING TWO MILLION MEGABITES OF INFORMATION THROUGH YOUR HOUSE PER SECOND. THIS WORKS BECAUSE OF AN OPTICAL FIBER NETWORK WE INSTALL IN YOUR WALLS. AND RIGHT NOW THE SYSTEM IS ON SALE AT THIRTY PERCENT OFF.

Does that get your full attention? Or, would this generate more desire for a burglar alarm system?

YOUR MOTHER GAVE YOU THAT RING WHEN YOU GOT MARRIED. HER MOTHER GAVE IT TO HER WHEN SHE GOT MARRIED. IT WAS HER HOPE THAT YOU'D GIVE IT TO YOUR DAUGHTER WHEN SHE GETS MARRIED.
     BUT THAT'S NOT GOING TO HAPPEN. BECAUSE RIGHT NOW A CREEP WITH A DRUG HABIT IS SELLING IT FOR LESS THAN $100. TOO BAD YOU MADE IT SO EASY FOR HIM. YOU HAD NO ALARM SYSTEM. ALL HE HAD TO DO

WAS BREAK A WINDOW IN THE BACK AND HE HAD FULL
ACCESS TO EVERYTHING IN YOUR HOUSE.

If you lived in a high-crime area, you'd be *on* and highly likely
to see or hear that spot. What emotions am I conjuring up here?
Certainly, we're using fear as an emotion here, but we're also conjuring guilt and shame. Shame on you for not protecting a priceless
family heirloom. It's your fault because it was stolen on your watch.
This approach would work much better than simply giving you
facts and figures about security system components. And I don't
even have to mention a sale price.

A FEW COMMON EMOTIONS

- Guilt
- Fear
- Anxiety
- Gratitude
- Envy
- Sorrow
- Pity
- Rage
- Frustration

- Disgust
- Lust
- Desire
- Elation
- Greed
- Anticipation
- Skepticism
- Responsibility

USE EMOTION TO MAKE AN ILLOGICAL
PURCHASE SEEM LOGICAL

Let's say I was trying to sell computers. I might again use guilt as an
emotion to reach parents. Perhaps something like this:

ARE YOU THE LAST FAMILY ON YOUR STREET THAT STILL
DOESN'T HAVE A COMPUTER FOR YOUR CHILDREN'S EDU-
CATION? SHAME ON YOU.

What I'm doing here is using guilt or shame as a motivator to get a person to make what appeared to be an illogical purchase seem logical and practical.

SLEEPING WITH MONSTERS?

I had a client who was selling allergy relief products. He said he had advertised some of the products in the paper, but there was little response to the ad. I looked at the ad—it mentioned a brand of allergy relief pillow and mattress covers that were supposed to keep dust mites off of you. The ad headline mentioned a discount on the covers. It went into some detail of product features, for example, that the covers were woven with special threads that were spaced "X" microns apart, to keep dust mites off of you. That, essentially, was the content of the ad. It was pretty boring. No wonder it didn't work.

When I asked the client what dust mites were, he said they were microscopic creatures that lived inside your pillow and mattress. When I asked him what they looked like, he pulled out an enlarged photo. They looked like monsters. I asked him how they caused allergies. He told me that every night while you sleep, millions of these dust mites come out of your pillow and mattress and crawl all over you, feeding on your dead skin cells.

I said, "Wow, and that causes your allergies?"

He said, "No, it's much worse than that."

"What could be worse?" I asked.

"Well, it's disgusting," he continued. "You see, it's their fecal matter."

I said, "You mean they poo-poo on you?"

"Yes," he continued. "And when you inhale the poo-poo, your allergies get bad.

Why? Do you think you could do something with this?" he asked. "Absolutely. In fact, I look forward to it," I said with a grin.

What emotions would you use to make a headline for your commercial in this case? I used fear and disgust. My target was fastidious women. The script began like this.

IT'S NOT A QUESTION OF WHO YOU'RE SLEEPING WITH EVERY NIGHT . . . BUT WHAT AND HOW MANY. EVERY NIGHT WHILE YOU SLEEP, MILLIONS OF DUST MITES . . . UP CLOSE THEY LOOK LIKE GIANT COCKROACHES . . . COME OUT OF YOUR PILLOW AND MATTRESS AND CRAWL ALL OVER YOU . . . FEEDING ON YOUR DEAD SKIN CELLS. BUT IT'S NOT THE DUST MITES THEMSELVES THAT CAUSE YOUR ALLERGIES . . . NO . . . IT'S MUCH WORSE THAN THAT . . . IT'S . . . HOW CAN I SAY THIS . . . IT'S THEIR . . . FECAL MATTER. (SFX WOMAN SCREAMING)

The rest of the script described the benefits of using the product, and we never had to discuss price. It worked. The client called and said he got a great response to the advertising. In this case, fear and disgust were excellent motivators to help the client sell his product.

USE AN EMOTIONAL HEADLINE IMMEDIATELY

Always use emotional headlines at the beginning of your spot. Do it right away. In fact, you must get the attention of members of your audience who are on for your client's product or service very quickly, or you will lose their attention.

When you discuss creative with a client, always try to put yourself in the shoes of the person who would buy your client's product or service. What emotion would you use to immediately get the attention of those people?

Emotional headlines work well when you're trying to get an appointment, as well. When you have trouble getting a client to return a call, try using guilt. Say something like, "Hello, this is [name] again. I called you a couple of times and you haven't returned my call. I must have done something or said something that offended you, but I can't imagine what that could have been. Could you please call me back and just tell me what I might have said or done to offend you so I won't make the same mistake again?"

There is logic in using the word "logic." Remember that people don't necessarily buy logically, but they want to think they are. The word "logical" seems to connote another word, "responsible." That's why I use the word "logical" often, when I'm making a presentation to a client. I'll make a point and then say, "Look, it's logical." You'll notice that many people automatically nod their heads when they hear that word, and a head nod is usually a buying signal. The word "logical" also works in commercials. Help your listeners or viewers make the decision to visit your client, because doing so is logical.

W o r k s h e e t: Making the Spot Emotional

You don't have to be a creative genius, but you *should at least* know and recognize the differences between good and bad advertising and you *should* be able to explain these differences to a client.

1. Write two headlines for existing clients. Remember to make them emotional headlines.

2. Think of the different emotions you can invoke in your spots. List several emotions and the client who might be a good fit for using each emotion as a headline.

CHAPTER

■■■ 12 ■■■

Solving Customer Problems
Without Clichés

The third creative rule is to focus on benefits and results, not clichés. Mastering the concepts in this chapter will give you tremendous insight into just how bad broadcast creative really is. Use this bad news to your advantage. You could improve the efficiency and effectiveness of most advertising by 80 percent (many commercials contain as much as 80 percent meaningless clichés), simply by removing clichés and replacing them with language that a listener or viewer who is *on* for the client's product or service could understand and relate to.

Remember that a good spot always contains three important elements. In the previous chapters we discussed the first two rules:

1. Establish the identifiable difference.
2. Start with an emotional headline.

In this chapter, we'll discuss the third rule:

3. Explain benefits and results to your listeners or viewers, without using clichés.

EXPLAIN BENEFITS AND RESULTS
TO THE LISTENERS OR VIEWERS, WITHOUT CLICHÉS

Again, by simply knowing the differences between good and bad advertising and then being capable of explaining those differences to your client, you become much more of a resource to your local direct clients. From what you learn in this chapter, you'll find holes in local business's advertising strategies that dinosaurs could walk through.

Our commercials are infested with advertising clichés—and recall that clichés are nothing more than worthless ad-speak. It's not just radio and television salespeople who are responsible for bad copy. Some of the biggest advertising agencies in the country are also writing ad-speak and diminishing the effectiveness of their client's advertising.

Webster's dictionary defines *cliché* as a "trite phrase or expression." I call clichés meaningless words or phrases that take up space and have no place in your client's advertising.

The third thing you must do in every commercial is explain benefits and results to your listeners or viewers, without using clichés. In other words, how will the listener or viewer directly benefit from coming to the client's business? Identify and solve consumer problems without using clichés. This rule ties into your client's USP or identifiable difference. Always sell the benefit or result, not the product or service, without using clichés that say things like, "Best service in town."

For example, exactly what does your client mean when she wants to say to your audience that she has the "best service in town"? Does she mean that if she's not there in twenty minutes, the call is free? Does she mean that if you drop it off, it will be ready in an hour? Because, if that's what "best service" really means, then why not explain it? Listeners or viewers who are *on* for one-hour service would appreciate hearing that. Listeners or viewers who are "on" for "If we're not there in twenty minutes, the call is free" would love to hear that from your client.

So when your client gives you a cliché benefit or result, dig a little and find out what he really means. Then in your copy, you can explain to your audience what's really in it for them, how they really win by calling or visiting your client. "Best service" alone means absolutely nothing. It's just a tired, empty cliché and we hear it over and over and over again.

The best commercials *identify* and *solve* consumer problems in language that your viewers or listeners with similar problems will immediately identify with.

For example, if you're working with an assisted living center as a client, you should understand that you may have listeners or viewers who are struggling with guilt over the thought of putting an elderly parent into a "home." Your commercial should immediately identify these guilt-ridden children of elderly parents and then help them solve their guilt problems. The commercial might point out, for example, that as much as you would love to have an elderly relative living with you in your house, that might not be in the best interest of the old person. If that person were to fall, who would be there to pick him or her up? If you tried, you might hurt yourself as well. What if he accidentally overdoses on a medication or gets confused about what medicines he should take at what time?

UNLIKE YOUR HOME, THE ASSISTED LIVING CENTER WAS SPECIFICALLY DESIGNED TO ALLOW GREATER MOBILITY FOR OUR RESIDENTS. OUR HALLWAYS ARE WIDER. THE RAILINGS MAKE IT EASIER TO GET AROUND. THERE ARE NO STAIRS IN OUR FACILITY. IN FACT, MOBILITY IS SO MUCH EASIER HERE FOR ELDERLY PEOPLE THAT MANY FIND THEY ARE WALKING AND EXERCISING MORE THAN THEY WERE BEFORE. OUR NURSES MAKE ABSOLUTELY CERTAIN THAT ALL MEDICATIONS ARE TAKEN ON TIME.

There is a huge market for low-priced furniture. Unfortunately, most furniture stores use cliché-riddled spots. But consider this scenario. Imagine a single parent struggling to get by. He or she has just gone through a divorce and one of the consequences is there is little furniture left in the house. This means that this individual seldom if ever entertains at home. Family get-togethers are always at someone else's house. The individual would love to host a holiday meal but is embarrassed because of the lack of furniture. A savvy furniture store should identify and solve this problem by speaking directly to people who have the problem.

> IF YOU DON'T HAVE MUCH FURNITURE OR IF YOU FEEL YOU DON'T HAVE NICE FURNITURE, YOU MIGHT NOT ENTERTAIN TOO MUCH. WHAT A SHAME. WOULDN'T IT BE NICE TO HAVE A BIG FAMILY MEAL AT YOUR HOUSE FOR A CHANGE, INSTEAD OF ALWAYS HAVING TO GO TO A RELA-TIVE'S HOUSE? WE CAN HELP YOU. AT DISCOUNT FURNI-TURE WE SELL VERY WELL MADE DINING ROOM TABLES AND CHAIRS. THEY ARE SOLID OAK. THEY WILL LAST MANY, MANY YEARS AND THEY LOOK TERRIFIC. AND THESE DINING SETS ARE VERY AFFORDABLE, SO THAT YOU CAN HAVE A NICE TABLE AND CHAIRS IN TIME FOR THIS HOLIDAY SEASON. IMAGINE HOW NICE IT WOULD BE TO ENTERTAIN AT YOUR HOUSE. AT DISCOUNT FURNITURE WE CAN HELP YOU DO THAT WITH VERY NICE, WELL-MADE AND INEXPENSIVE FURNITURE.

In order for a spot to work properly, every word needs to be meaningful and contribute toward the goal of getting the listener or viewer to do business with the client. But instead, we are sabotaging the client's message (and ultimately our relationship with the client) by loading up their spots with these trite and meaningless clichés.

Here are some common advertising clichés.

COMMON CLICHÉS

- Call our staff of professionals
- Talk to our knowledgeable, trained staff
- Come see our friendly staff of professionals
- You'll love our loyal, dedicated employees

- Talk to our top-notch sales staff
- (Eight) convenient locations to better serve you
- Best service in town
- Serving (your town) since 1995
- Dedicated to serve you
- Service second to none
- Our motto is to serve you
- Working hard to serve you better
- The best kept secret in town
- For all of your needs
- Hurry in today
- But hurry . . . with prices like these, selection won't last long
- Your premier (product or service) headquarters
- Your low-price headquarters
- Choose from a wide variety of . . .
- It's a holiday tradition . . .
- Save on a wide selection of . . .
- Our loss is your gain
- We're slashing prices to the bone
- You've got to see it to believe it
- Where the customer is king
- We're saving the best for you
- Your low-cost leader
- Come visit our beautiful, spacious showroom
- We've got the wheels and the deals
- You can count on us for the friendliest deal in town

But wait . . . there's more . . .

- Shop the best and leave the rest to us.
- This is it!

- It's our red-tag event!
- Just in time for the holidays . . .
- We just can't be beat
- We guarantee the lowest prices
- We've withstood the test of time
- We're tried and true
- Everything drastically reduced just in time for this sale
- It's our biggest sales event of the year
- We'll shoot straight with you
- We're number one
- You'll save like never before
- Check out the deals we have in store for you
- We guarantee the lowest price or else!
- Prices have never been lower
- Unheard of
- Unbelievable
- The sales event of the decade
- Family owned and operated
- Time is running out
- Plus . . .
- Everybody's talking about it
- Huge selection
- But only for a limited time
- Everything must go
- We're declaring war on high prices
- This is one sale you don't want to miss
- We've lost our lease
- Sizzling red-hot summer sales event!
- You'll want to bring the whole family
- Free balloons and popcorn for the kids
- We won't be undersold

- A (your town) institution
- Not to mention our great food and happy hour specials
- Plenty of eager salespeople to assist you
- Midnight Madness

We've heard clichés so many times in radio and television spots that they literally "go in one ear and out the other," to use a cliché. Most people are so accustomed to hearing clichés in spots that they actually believe that's the way a spot is supposed to sound. And that's why most spots sound the same and don't stand out. Instead of "best service in town," you could say something like,

WHEN YOU CALL AAA PLUMBING, WE GUARANTEE THAT WE'LL BE AT YOUR DOOR TO FIX YOUR PROBLEM WITHIN TWENTY MINUTES OF YOUR CALL OR IT'S FREE.

As media reps, we should be asking ourselves every day, "How hard am I making it for our audience to do business with this client?" Wouldn't you agree that if you produced the advertiser's spot in a foreign language that it would be much more difficult for the audience to understand your client's message? Well, that's what we do when we use clichés in our spots. We're trying to communicate in a language that no one really speaks.

DON'T BE A CRAPMASTER!

Consider this scenario. The broadcast salesperson finally convinces the client to buy a schedule on his station.

Client: "Okay, okay . . . I'll buy it. But what are we going to do about the copy?"

Salesperson: "Yes sir, I'll help you with the copy. You know, I've been in the media sales business for six years now. In fact, I've been through three murders and executions."

Client: "You mean mergers and acquisitions."

Salesperson: "Yes, that's what I mean. And, I'm highly qualified to make your commercial. You see, I'm an expert at taking bits and pieces of crap from this list of clichés and putting them together with other bits of crap, so that you'll have a commercial that looks and sounds just like every other commercial."

Client: "Gee. You could do all of that for me?"

Salesperson: "Yes sir. You see, I'm a certified crapmaster. The best in town."

Client: "A crapmaster? Man, that sounds impressive. Well, be sure to put my business hours in that spot, even though they're the same as everybody else's. And don't forget that we are family owned and operated."

Broadcast people always laugh at the above scenario. Why? Because sadly, it's pretty darned close to the truth. Unfortunately, the truth has serious consequences that affect our pocketbooks. When the crapmaster spot fails to deliver, the client cancels and blames the medium or your station.

"Okay," you say. "This copy thing really is a serious issue. But how can I be sure that there is no crap in my copy?" I'm glad you asked. Just use a simple test on every single piece of copy you write. Mastering this test will be one of the most significant things you do in becoming a creative expert.

USE THE BEST FRIEND TEST ON YOUR COPY

If you don't believe what I'm saying, just use the best friend test on every piece of copy. If you wouldn't say those *exact same words* to your best friend, then they have no place in your spot.

For example, could you imagine yourself saying to your best friend, "(friend's name), this is one sizzling red-hot summer sale we can't afford to miss! They'll have plenty of loyal and eager salespeople to assist us and their service is second to none! But, time is running out. We'll love their beautiful and spacious showroom and their holiday cheer. Plus, their prices just can't be beat! But only for a limited time and only at participating stores!" If you said that to somebody, she would think that you had lost your mind. However, you'll hear it over and over and over in the average radio or tv commercial.

REMEMBER TO USE THE BLANK SHEET OF PAPER TEST ON YOUR CLIENTS

Make your client aware of all of the ad-speak his competitors are running. Here is where you could use that blank sheet of white paper and ask the client, "If you were trying to sell this sheet of white paper, would it make sense to hold it up against a white background or a black background?" Of course, it would make sense to hold it up against a black background in order to stand out. In other words, for a commercial to be effective, it must stand out from the other commercials on the station.

COLLECT CLICHÉS

Start becoming a student in the difference between good and bad advertising. Be a student of bad advertising. That means that you should listen critically to radio and television advertising and watch and listen for clichés. When you hear one, repeat it to yourself and smile. Because once you get really good at recognizing the waste we have in commercial scripts, you'll look like an advertising genius to your clients. You won't believe all of the ad-speak you'll hear and see when you really start paying careful attention. You'll find that almost every spot you see or hear will be loaded with stupid clichés.

Clients always appreciate listening to somebody who could help them increase the efficiency and effectiveness of the advertising they are spending their hard-earned money on. Your knowledge about the money businesses are wasting on clichés will help you get more appointments. Every time you see, hear, or read cliché-infested ads, you can smile and tell yourself, "There's another client who needs my expertise."

Again, you could back up the claim that you could improve the effectiveness and efficiency of advertising your client is already doing by 80 percent, simply by removing cliché ad-speak and replacing it with benefits and results that your listeners or viewers would really care about. Collect advertising clichés. It's a lot cheaper than collecting cars or jewelry. Take the list of clichés I'm providing for you here and add to it when you hear new ones. Become an evangelist with this knowledge. Go out and show your clients how they could outsmart their competitors by writing more effective and efficient scripts.

NO MORE WALLPAPER SPOTS

A spot that looks like or sounds like a spot is camouflage. And nowadays, where the average person is inflicted with a minimum of 5,000 commercial impressions per day, camouflage means sabotage. Tell your clients that we don't want a spot that sounds or looks like a spot. If the spot is different, it will stand out. If a spot is not out-standing, it won't stand out at all. Use the "Best Friend Test" on every single piece of your copy.

W o r k s h e e t: Solving Consumer Problems Without Clichés

Become an expert on ad-speak and the other creative elements we've discussed so far. As a creative expert you have an identifiable difference from the chiquitas in your market.

1. Name three important elements of a good spot:

    a.

    b.

    c.

Review the spots written below.

THIS IS ONE SALE YOU DON'T WANT TO MISS. AT BERRING FORD IN BELVUE WE MUST SELL TWO HUNDRED UNITS THIS MONTH. WE'RE OUT OF SPACE AND MUST MAKE ROOM FOR NEW INVENTORY. SO WE'RE DOING WHAT-EVER IT TAKES TO GET YOU INTO A NEW FORD. YOU'LL WANT TO CHECK OUT ALL OF OUR RED-TAG SPECIALS. SAVE HUNDREDS, EVEN THOUSANDS OFF MSRP. COME TO BERRING FORD TODAY AND TALK TO ONE OF OUR KNOWLEDGEABLE SALES STAFF. YOU'LL LOVE OUR BEAU-TIFUL AND SPACIOUS SHOWROOM AND REMEMBER, AT BERRING IN BELVUE, WE'VE GOT THE WHEELS AND THE DEALS. PUSH, PULL, OR DRAG YOUR CURRENT RIDE TO BERRING FORD. WE'RE PAYING TOP DOLLAR FOR YOUR TRADE. AT BERRING FORD IN BELVUE WE WILL SELL TWO HUNDRED UNITS THIS MONTH DURING THIS ONCE-IN-A-LIFETIME RED-TAG SALES EVENT. WHEN YOU SHOP BERRING YOU WIN EVERY TIME. BERRING FORD   ON HWY. 8 IN BELVUE. BERRING FORD . . . WE'VE GOT THE WHEELS AND THE DEALS.

Husband: HI HONEY, I'M HOME.

Wife: OH, HONEY . . . WELL, WHILE YOU WERE GONE I HEARD ABOUT THE DEAL OF A LIFETIME.

Husband: REALLY? WHAT WAS IT?

Wife: WELL, BY SIMPLY STOPPING BY JONES FLOORING NEAR THE MALL AT 1107 HARDY STREET WE CAN SAVE OVER 40 PERCENT ON NEW CARPET FOR OUR HOME.

Husband: BOY, THAT IS A GOOD DEAL. WITH NEW CAR-PET WE'LL FINALLY HAVE THE HOME OF OUR DREAMS.

Wife: THAT'S RIGHT. PLUS, WE'LL GET THE BENEFIT OF OVER FIFTEEN YEARS OF EXPERT CARPET ADVICE FROM ONE OF JONES FLOORING'S FRIENDLY AND EXPERIENCED SALES STAFF. IN FACT, WE'LL LOVE THE WHOLE JONES FAMILY. FATHER RICK, WIFE JESSE, AND THEIR SONS ED AND RICK ALL WORK THERE.

Husband: SOUNDS LIKE JONES CARPET COULD BE THE BEST KEPT SECRET IN TOWN. SO, LET'S GO.

Wife: WE'D BETTER HURRY . . . WITH THIS UP TO 40 PERCENT OFF SELECTION WON'T LAST LONG.

ANNCR: JONES FLOORING . . . 1107 HARDY NEAR THE MALL. JONES FLOORING . . . YOUR LOW-PRICED FAMILY OWNED AND OPERATED CARPET HEADQUARTERS SINCE 1991.

AT DUNAGAN'S FURNITURE OUTLET WE'VE LOST OUR LEASE. THAT MEANS INSTANT SAVINGS ON FURNITURE FOR THE WHOLE HOME. LIVING ROOM . . . DINING ROOM . . . BEDROOM . . . DEN AND OFFICE. EVERYTHING IN THE STORE MUST GO. AND JUST IN TIME FOR THE HOLIDAYS. YOU'LL SAVE LIKE NEVER BEFORE ON CHAIRS, TABLES, COUCHES . . . EVEN COMPUTER DESKS. OUR LEASE IS UP AND THAT MEANS WE'RE OUTTA HERE. DINING ROOM SETS SLASHED UP TO SIXTY PERCENT. SAVE HUNDREDS ON BEDROOM SETS. THIS IS ONE SALE YOU DON'T WANT TO MISS. HUGE SELECTION. AND WITH PRICES LIKE THESE, SELECTION WON'T LAST LONG. YOU'VE GOT TO SEE THESE PRICES TO BELIEVE THEM. IT'S THE DUNAGAN'S FURNITURE OUTLET'S LOST OUR LEASE SALES EVENT AND OUR LOSS IS YOUR GAIN. CHECK OUT DUNAGAN'S FURNITURE OUTLET ON MANOR ROAD TODAY AND SAVE LIKE NEVER BEFORE ON ALL OF YOUR FURNITURE NEEDS.

2. Using the "Best Friend Test," count the cliches in the three spots. How many cliches in spot #1 can you identify? How about spots #2 and #3?

3. Name two local direct accounts on your list that are currently running crapmaster copy.

CHAPTER

■■■ 13 ■■■

Telling Your Target Market
What to Do

There is no question that creative knowledge means power in this business and distinguishes you from not only chiquitas at the other stations, but also from rinky-dink little crapmaster advertising agencies. Most of these parasitic goobers don't know anywhere near as much as you do when it comes to the difference between a good and bad spot. If you don't believe me, just pay attention to some of their commercials. Little podunk agency creative is usually infested with clichés.

So far, we've discussed the following elements in writing good advertising scripts:

1. Establish an identifiable difference.
2. Come up with an emotional headline.
3. Explain benefits and results to your listeners or viewers without using clichés.

Now, we'll go over the fourth and final element and wrap up this section on the difference between good and bad advertising.

4. Make sure that your client's call to action is crystal clear.

A GOOD SPOT HAS A SPECIFIC CALL TO ACTION

The fourth and final element we must communicate in a good spot is the call to action. The call to action is precisely what it says—what the client wants the listener or viewer to do. Our job is to make sure that the client's call to action is crystal clear for our audience. Unfortunately, we regularly mess this part up and that's a big mistake. Here's an example of how easy it is to mess up the call-to-action. "That number again is 484-2597. Family owned and operated since 1967." Even if you're *on* for what the client is selling, how difficult is the crapmaster making it to remember the telephone number? 2-5-9-7? Or was that 1-9-6-7? What in the heck was the number? How difficult is the crapmaster making it for the listeners or viewers to do business with the client? Pretty darned hard if the audience member can't remember the client's phone number or the client's address or the client's website. For this reason the call to action must be the very last line in the script. Never follow the call to action with anything else, especially a cliché slogan.

ONE CALL TO ACTION IS BETTER THAN TWO OR THREE

If your client is in a service-oriented business like plumbing, there is no reason to direct your listeners or viewers to the client's physical address. The client does not want your listeners or viewers driving to her location and seeing all of the old toilets out in the front yard. The phone number in this case is the only call to action you'd need to emphasize. You'd want to repeat that phone number frequently and remember that the phone number would also appear as the last thing written in the spot. If a client wants people to come to her business location, obviously you'd mention the address frequently. There would be no need to mention a phone number. If the client wants listeners or viewers to go to his website, you would teach your audience the website. You will confuse listeners and viewers by trying to teach them multiple calls to action.

COMPLICATED ADDRESSES

What if the client's location is not easy to find, or his location is hard to describe? Location problems mean marketing problems for your client. You would be very wise to advise your client that you are aware that he has a marketing problem, but you will do what you can to guide your audience to his address.

In a case of a difficult-to-find location, I might begin my script by pointing out the biggest intersection or landmark closest to my client's business. "Can you visualize the intersection of Manchaca at William Cannon Drive? Can you see that intersection in your mind?"

What about situations when the client does not want to use a famous landmark to make his or her location easier to find, because it "cheapens" the business? I usually tell the client to get over it. Why doesn't the client try draping a huge camouflaged tarp over his neighbor? That landmark, perhaps a box store or a fast food franchise, is probably not going to go away. Get over it and use the landmark. The idea is to make it as easy as possible to get to the client's business.

On television, I can keep a map up on the screen. But I must also *tell* viewers how to get to the client's business. Why? Because many people "watch" television from a different room. They're listening, so vocalize the call to action at the end of the television spot to give these people a chance to hear the location or phone number.

COMPLICATED PHONE NUMBERS

Vanity phone numbers are just wonderful. We should call them memory numbers instead, because that's exactly what they are. I had a client in the carpet and upholstery cleaning business who had the number 47 CLEAN. I asked him how he got the number and he told me it was the best $300 he'd ever spent. He just called the number. It turned out to be a residential listing. He told the homeowner that he'd give him $300 for his phone number. The homeowner said, "Heck yeah!" He had no idea that his phone number spelled 47 CLEAN.

"Call 4-PIZZAS," would be much easier to remember than some random number. If vanity phone numbers are available in your area, the phone company will help your client get one. Several offer free searches for vanity numbers. For example, Verizon has one at http://www.22.verizon.com/Vanity/.

Tell your client that it is logical to make his phone number as easy as possible to remember. Encourage your client to get a vanity telephone number, because logically, he needs a number that is as easy as possible for your listeners or viewers to remember.

If for some reason vanity numbers are not available in your area, teach your listeners or viewers the hardest part first. Here's how that works. Let's say the number is 474-9016. There are fewer prefixes in a market than there are suffixes. Some markets might have fewer than fifty telephone number prefixes. But there are thousands of possible combinations for suffixes. So, teach the suffix first, then the prefix. The spot would work something like this:

THIS IMPORTANT FIRE SAFETY INFORMATION IS BROUGHT TO YOU BY QUALITY ELECTRIC. STATISTICS PROVE THAT THIRTY PERCENT OF ALL HOUSE FIRES START WITH AN ELECTRICAL PROBLEM. IF YOU WANT TO AVOID FIRES IN YOUR HOME, REMEMBER NINETY-SIXTEEN. IF YOU'VE NOTICED LIGHTS THAT ARE DIMMING WHEN THEY'RE NOT SUPPOSED TO, YOU MIGHT HAVE AN ELECTRICAL PROBLEM. REMEMBER NINETY-SIXTEEN. IF YOU HAVE ELECTRICAL OUTLETS THAT AREN'T WORKNG ANY MORE, YOU HAVE A POTENTIAL ELECTRICAL FIRE. NINETY-SIXTEEN. IF YOUR HOME WAS BUILT MORE THAN FORTY YEARS AGO, YOUR ELECTRICAL SYSTEM COULD BE FAULTY AND THAT COULD RESULT IN YOUR HOUSE CATCHING ON FIRE. NINETY-SIXTEEN. CALL 474-NINETY-SIXTEEN AND A LICENSED QUALITY ELECTRICIAN WILL LOCATE AND REPAIR AN ELEC-TRICAL PROBLEM BEFORE IT TURNS INTO A FIRE. CALL QUALITY ELECTRIC NOW AT 474- (PAUSE) NINETY-SIXTEEN.

The pause before the last suffix helps the listener or viewer to mentally state the last numbers for you, further entrenching the telephone number into his or her memory. Many larger markets have a variety of area codes, which further complicate the call to action problem. Just remember that there are far fewer area codes than there are prefixes. You would teach the number the same way, starting with the suffix. Then introduce the prefix. And in the very last line, introduce the area code.

When dealing with phone numbers, you might want to refer listeners or viewers to the white pages of the phone book. In other words, you might say, "Call 474-ninety-sixteen or look up Quality Electric in the White Pages." Don't refer your audience to the Yellow Pages, because when a person goes to the Yellow Pages, he or she will then have the opportunity to shop all of your client's competitors.

Finally, when dealing with phone numbers, you might be able to say, "Call 474-ninety-sixteen or call this station and ask for the telephone number of Quality Electric." If your station management doesn't have a problem with your receptionist giving out client telephone numbers, this method might be a terrific way to help your client with his phone number problem.

WHEN A WEBSITE IS THE CALL TO ACTION

We estimate that there are anywhere from one to six billion pages on the Internet right now. If your client's call to action is a website, then make it easier, not harder for your viewers or listeners to go to your client's site. You do not have to say, "Go to http slash slash www" any more. I still hear that on occasion and it's a complete waste of time. Just say, "Go to greatpizza.com," for example, and people will know what to do.

But rather than saying, "Go to," I have another idea for you. Provided that your copy gives your audience compelling reasons to do so, tell your viewers or listeners to bookmark your client's website. Tell them to "bookmark greatpizza.com," for example. Typically, people bookmark fewer than fifty websites. If I were your client, I think I'd rather be one of fifty than one of four billion.

One more thing regarding websites: If your client has a website, then he or she should have no trouble with buying overnight or weekend spots from you. Because if a client has a website, he's open 24 hours a day, 7 days a week.

WRAPPING IT UP

The concepts for good broadcast creative are really easy, aren't they?

1. Establish an identifiable difference.
2. Start with an emotional headline.
3. Discuss benefits and results without clichés.
4. Make the call-to-action crystal clear.

If you mess up just one of these four rules, you might destroy the entire campaign.

SIDE NOTES ON CREATIVE

As you consider your script and production, think about some of these things.

- Avoid two-voice skits. They hardly ever turn out the way you think they will. They usually wind up looking or sounding fake and hokey and unprofessional.
- Big disc jockey voices are cliché. We always have the same two or three big voices doing all of our spots. Hardly anyone really talks that way. Instead, whenever you can, use real people in your spots, either satisfied customers or business owners. These people are usually evangelists, with strong beliefs in the client's product or service. Their enthusiasm is infectious and helps create desire in listeners or viewers who are *on* for what

your client is trying to sell. But don't allow them to read scripts. Instead, ask provocative questions. You'll get real answers from real people, the way real people really talk. Leave in an occasional speech error, like an "um" or two. It makes the subject of your spot sound even more normal and real. Remember, the idea is to create spots that do not look like or sound like wallpaper crapmaster spots.

- Do jingles really work to build mindshare for a local direct advertiser? My answer is generally yes. Jingles can be a great way to stuff a brand into the heads of unsuspecting listeners. But on the other hand, jingles could be detrimental to an advertising campaign if you fail to follow some simple rules. Let's look at why jingles do and do not work. Last year while touring the beautiful zoo in Sydney, Australia, I met a local couple near the death adder cage. We struck up a conversation and they asked me what I did for a living. When I told them I worked in broadcast advertising, the woman said, "Oh, we just hate Australian media. It is those damned jingles! They drive us crazy. Our children sing them all the time!"

Some jingles just never go away. Some seem stuck in my head forever, even though they are not broadcast any more, and some are so old that the product doesn't even exist any more. Jingles pop into your head at the worst times and they just will not go away. Here are some old jingles that I still remember, whether I want to or not.

"Dirt can't hide from intensified Tide."

"When it says Libby's Libby's Libby's on the label, label, label."

"Oh, I wish I were an Oscar Mayer wiener."

"Winston tastes good. like a cigarette should."

"You'll look better in a sweater washed in Woolite."

"You deserve a break today at McDonald's."

"Coca-Cola. Coca-Cola for extra fun get more than one, buy an extra carton of Coke."

"Call Roto-Rooter . . . that's the name . . . and away go troubles down the drain." That is good branding, and when my drain or toilet is clogged, the name Roto-Rooter definitely comes to mind. It is an easy jingle to remember and it is easy to sing.

Yes, good jingles stick and they sometimes work for local clients as well. I said sometimes. Here are the reasons that many jingles do not work.

- The average person can't sing them. Jingles don't work when they have too many notes. Logically, it's hard to learn a song that's hard to learn. Good jingles only cover a few notes. Keep it simple, stupid.
- Jingles don't work as well if I cannot reach certain notes in that jingle. Good jingles keep the notes in a short range that most anybody could sing.
- Jingles do not work if the lyrics are hard to learn. Again, keep it simple, stupid.
- You cannot learn a jingle if you don't hear it. Jingles only work with frequency. I can't learn a song unless I hear it a lot.
- Jingles also need time to embed. Many media salespeople are reluctant to sell jingle packages to their clients because they think that money toward a jingle cuts into a budget that should be spent on the schedule. In fact, that's very short-sighted when you consider the longer term ramifications. The most successful jingles run month after month, year after year. So as an account executive, I love a good jingle package. In order to get the song properly established in the minds of listeners, a client invests in commercial music; however, he must also invest in a long-term schedule with heavy frequency. One of the best things about a good jingle is the fact that once it's well established, it immediately embeds the client's brand, even if the listener switches stations right after the song begins playing.

A good local jingle package usually runs under $3,500. That price usually includes a full-sing :60 and :30, donut versions (a jingle with a :30-:45 second hole for copy), and short intros and stings. In a word, yes. I do like jingles, and I think they can be extremely effective in branding a client into your listeners' and viewers' heads. But make sure that you are using a jingle company that understands and uses the rules we discussed.

Despite the fact that jingles work so well and we remember them for so long, we are hearing fewer of them in commercials for national brands. Instead, we hear more hit records in commercials. Led Zeppelin in Cadillac spots, for example. That's a shame, because good jingles do a better job than classic rock tunes when it comes to teaching us about specific product benefits and results.

W o r k s h e e t: Telling Your Target Market What to Do

For a spot to work properly, every word needs to be meaningful and contribute toward the goal of getting the listener to do business with the client.

Use the following information to create a script. Make sure that you come up with a USP. Then write an EMOTIONAL HEADLINE, followed by BENEFITS AND RESULTS WITHOUT CLICHÉS. Make sure that your CALL TO ACTION is crystal clear and repeated.

a. **Client:** Mason's Auto Repair

b. **Address:** 1121 North I-35 near Starbuck's

c. **Unique features:** caters to a largely female audience, extensive references, foreign and domestic repair, free shuttle, stays open late till 8 pm, one day service in most cases.

PART

■■■ III ■■■

Demonstrating That Using Your Station Is Not a Gamble, but a Good Calculated Risk

CHAPTER

■■■ 14 ■■■

Calculating Return on Investment (ROI) and Managing Client Expectations

MANAGING THE CLIENT'S EXPECTATIONS

Do you, with every single local direct client in every single case, ask what his or her average sale and gross profit margin are? If you don't, then you're selling blind. And you face the risk of being blindsided.

This concept of return on investment may change the way you sell forever. Remember that knowledge is power in this business. Armed with certain pieces of client information, you could make huge strides toward completely managing your client's expectations about results. This is important, because except for horrible creative, the other typical reason that a client says, "I tried it once and it didn't work," is because you and the client were never on the same page regarding how many of your listeners or viewers should respond to the client's message.

If you're sick of surprise cancellations, if you're sick of having to give away bonus spots, if you're sick of missing sales because you're not rated number one or hearing "I don't like your music or programming on your station," you'll *love* these chapters on Return on Investment (ROI). If you'd like to double or triple what your client thinks he should be spending with you and if you'd like more long-term contracts from clients, then you'll want to pay very careful attention to this series on how to calculate and explain ROI.

In this chapter, we work on ways to determine how much money your client should really be spending with you, not how much the client "thinks" he should be "gambling" on your station. Why would we leave something that important up to chance?

HOW DO I DETERMINE HOW MUCH MY CLIENT SHOULD BE SPENDING?

Unfortunately, it's true that most local direct budgets for radio and television stations come out of thin air. When you ask salespeople how they determined the budget they suggest to a client, most say, "Well, that's just what I thought the client could afford to spend." You *thought* that's what the client wanted to spend? You didn't work through an ROI calculation with the client, did you? So essentially you're saying that you just pulled that number out of your rear end?

The other answer to the budget question is usually, "That's what the client says his budget is." Of course my next question would be, "Where did the client come up with that budget?" Again, is it possible that the client is also pulling the budget out of thin air? Absolutely. Especially if the client perceives that he "tried it once and it didn't work." Or, is the budget actually based on some type of ROI calculation?

EXAMPLE

When I approach a new client and work out an ROI calculation, I generally start with what it would cost to own some significant "real estate" on my station. That is, to own one or more days, or to own several spots per week in a day-part, or to own more than one spot in a particular program.

Let's say we're talking to a furniture store. Assume in this case that I work for a radio station with a weekly CUME (cumulative weekly audience, the biggest number of different listeners or viewers you have in a week) audience of 100,000. My average rate is $100. I have no idea what the client's budget is, but I'd like to see this client running at least thirty spots a week on my station. That way, the client could really own two or three days on my station. For example, I could cluster those spots over a two-day period with fifteen spots per day. Or, I might really dominate a specific day-part over a week's time. The point is to start with a big number of spots per week, not a small number.

I'm speaking to the decision maker. "Mr. Client, they say we reach about 100,000 consumers a week. Now, I'm not saying we could reach everybody on our station with your advertising. That would be impossible. To do that, we'd have to run the same spot every minute of every hour of every day. Then, of course, nobody would listen to our station any more. But the point is we don't have to reach everybody. We're just trying to reach a percentage of our listeners who are *on* for a furniture purchase this week. Since our demographic is the same as the one you're trying to reach, then it's logical and statistically sound that we have listeners who will buy furniture from you or one of your competitors this week. We need to reach those people and also begin branding those people who aren't *on* for new furniture this week, but might be *on* in the future.

"Let's just say, for example, that you were spending $3,000 per week on our station (I always start high, you can always come down and it's harder to go up). What is your average sale here in the store?"

- **Average sale:** The dollar total of all of the sales from an average day, divided by the number of sales written or rung up.

The client responds that his average sale is about $800. And, what is the gross profit margin in the furniture business?

- **Gross profit margin:** The percentage of profit AFTER the business has paid for materials (retail outlet) or labor (service-oriented business) only. GPM is calculated by subtracting either the cost of labor or the cost of materials, but not both, from the sales price. Gross profit does not include rent, utilities, salaries, taxes or any other expenses. Including those factors would give you *net* profit. And if I asked a client what his *net* profit was, he'd probably tell me that was none of my business. But gross profit is a fair question, because it's virtually the same for every business in your client's particular product or service category. For example, many retail establishments operate on what we call "keystone," or a 50 percent gross profit margin. Clothiers and jewelers would buy an item from a manufacturer and then mark it up 100 percent to sell in their store. So when you subtract the cost of goods, you get a 50 percent gross profit margin.

Gross profit margin (GPM) in the furniture business is 40 percent. GPM for an appliance dealer is about 35 percent. GPM for a restaurant could run as high as 70 percent, depending on food cost. GPM at a nightclub is about 70 percent. For a manufactured homes dealer, GPM is 40 percent. Don't confuse gross profit margin with net profit.

The furniture client says his gross profit margin is about 40 percent. That would mean that the client is making about $320 gross profit on an average sale of $800. At this point I can do the math and determine that in order to get close to breakeven for this $3,000 campaign, the spots on my station would need to stimulate roughly ten sales for the client ($320 gross profit/sale × 10 sales = $3,200). Is that possible?

With a good spot that breaks through the "craposphere" of all of the other bad furniture store commercials, and with a good, solid schedule, it seems like a good calculated risk that I could catch ten fish out of my lake of 100,000 listeners per week. In fact, those ten fish would only represent .01 percent of my total weekly audience.

ASK FOR MORE

At this point, I might suggest to my client that we might "cast the bait" a few more times on this lake and perhaps go for twenty furniture customers. Heck, twenty customers still seem like a good calculated risk on our station. That would only represent .02 percent of our weekly audience. And I'll bet that with sixty "casts" with that good "bait," we just might be able to catch at least twenty new furniture customers.

KNOW YOUR STATION'S CUME NUMBER

Your CUME number is the biggest ratings number you've got. It's not households, it's people. CUME is the total number of different people that tune in to your station in a typical week. If you don't know your CUME number, ask your sales manager.

NOT IN A RATED MARKET?

Then try to come up with a number that you and the client both agree is fair. Take the entire population of your signal coverage area. Tell the client that obviously you market your station and that a percentage of that population tunes in on a weekly basis. Establish a fair percentage.

STOP WINGING IT WITH BUDGETS
AND CLIENT EXPECTATIONS

Stop recommending schedule amounts to clients without working out an ROI calculation first. You can't blame anybody but yourself when a client's expectations about results are not logical or you're not getting as much budget as you should be getting from your client.

What you can do is educate and manage expectations and increase your budget by knowing what the client's **average sale** and **gross profit margin** are. Use those numbers against your station's CUME and show the client that using your station looks like a good calculated risk. It's easy and it's logical.

W o r k s h e e t: Calculating Return on Investment (ROI) and Managing Client Expectations

By explaining return on investment (ROI), you will teach your clients that your campaign looks like a very good calculated risk.

1. Before reading this chapter, how were you managing your client's expectations about advertising results?

2. Explain in your own words how you would coach a client through an ROI calculation on your station.

3. Think of the names of two clients to whom you will be presenting this week. You should know the average sale and gross profit margin for each of those two clients. You should also know your station's 12-plus weekly CUME audience figure and your station's average rate. Now, based on a twenty-spot schedule on your station, determine how many average sales your client would have to make in order to break even on your advertising campaign.

   12-Plus Weekly CUME _____   Station's Average Rate _____
   Client #1
   Average Sale ____ Gross Profit Margin ____ Break even # ____
   Client #2
   Average Sale ____ Gross Profit Margin ____ Break even # ____

CHAPTER
■■■ 15 ■■■

Explaining the Pure Logic of Buying Your Station

HOW TO EXPLAIN ROI TO A LOCAL DIRECT CLIENT

Let's say you're working with a jewelry store. The client's average sale for an engagement ring is $1,500. His gross profit margin is keystone, or 50 percent. How many rings would you have to sell for this jeweler to break even on your little bitty $3,000 weekly schedule?

The client owns a funeral home. Its average sale is $7,000. Gross profit margin for funeral homes is a whopping 55 percent (if the client doesn't know his industry gross margin of profit, contact his professional association and ask for the information). How many funerals would you have to sell for the client in order to justify your little measly $10,000 weekly schedule?

The client is a homebuilder. His average sale is $160,000. His gross profit margin is 23 percent. How many new homes must the builder sell in order to justify your little puny, piddly little $15,000 weekly schedule?

ROI knowledge means power for you in negotiating with local direct clients. If you're not using this concept every time you call on a local direct client, you're nuts and you're going to get nasty surprises from clients who think that your station "isn't working."

Most broadcast salespeople have never fully understood and used an ROI calculation with clients and shame on us. Because of our industry's lack of understanding of this very important part of the sales process, radio and televisions stations have had to sacrifice billions of dollars in lost sales, wasted time, and sales department turnover. That doesn't include the billions more we have wasted in needless bonus spots just to keep dissatisfied clients on the air, all because we were never on the same page as the client about measurable results from campaigns on our stations. In Mexico, they call bonus spots "bonificacion." I find that highly ironic since we in the broadcast business are the ones getting—well, let's move on.

This chapter further illustrates the urgency of managing client expectations with an ROI calculation. It also covers rate resistance, where it comes from and how to deal with it.

AN INTERESTING SITUATION

The owner of a mobile home dealership decided he was ready to "give a radio station a try." He said he was even prepared to spend $2,000 on a schedule (the average rate on the station was around $100) and that this was his first experience with a radio station in several years. He said the last time he tried using radio it "didn't work," so "it had better work this time."

The account manager asked what the retailer's average sale was. The client replied, "$60,000." "What's your gross profit margin?" asked the account executive. The client told him it was about 30 percent. The account exec then asked how many $60,000 sales he would have to make to justify the $2,000 he was going to spend on the station. The client responded, "Oh, maybe a dozen."

"Twelve?" the AE asked incredulously. "I mean, how many individual $60,000 sales must you make in order to actually pay for our $2,000 weekly radio schedule?"

"Well, I guess fewer than a dozen," said the client. Yes, much fewer than a dozen.

After a little more discussion, the manager and the client agreed that they would have to attract a minimum of **one** new buying customer in order wind up with over 1,000 percent return on advertising investment. That's quite a difference.

The sales manager went on to explain that the station had about 150,000 listeners per week. He reminded the client that we weren't trying to reach everybody, we don't have to do that. But what if, with a good commercial and a logical schedule, just 1 percent of the station's audience responded to the client's message? How many people would that be?

1% of weekly CUME = 1,500 customers

The manager said, "It's not likely that that's going to happen. But what if just one-half of one percent of the audience responded to a good spot and a logical schedule, how many people would that be?

1/2 of 1% of weekly CUME = 750 customers

"Probably not going to happen," said the sales manager. But, what if just one-fourth of one-percent of our audience responded?

1/4 of 1% of weekly CUME = 375 customers

You see where this is going now. Let's take it further.

1/8 of 1% of weekly CUME =187 customers
1/16 of 1% = 94
1/32 of 1% = 47
1/64 of 1% = 23

1/128 of 1% = 12
1/256 of 1% = 6
1/512 of 1% = 3
1/1024 of 1 % =1.5

What was the magic number that the account manager and the client agreed upon? JUST ONE!

In order to break even on the advertising campaign, the client would only need to effectively reach 1/1024 of 1 percent of our audience. The station's format matched the client's demographic. The dealership had no perceptible marketing problems, so the odds looked good. To the client, the advertising campaign now appeared to be a good calculated risk.

MANAGE THE CLIENT'S EXPECTATIONS

At this point, the account executive suggested that with those numbers it would seem like a pretty good calculated risk to increase the budget and go for three average sales. The client wound up agreeing to double the budget to go for two new customers.

The schedule ran. This was the only advertising the client did for this particular sale. He tallied a total of four customers responding to the advertising and spending a minimum of $60,000 each. The client was ecstatic. But what if the client and the account exec had never had that conversation? What if the campaign had run and only attracted four people spending a minimum of $60,000? The client would have said that the campaign was a failure. And his perception would have been based on nothing more than a preconceived notion about how many people (a dozen?) he thought should respond to the advertising campaign.

THE CLIENT'S PERCEPTION IS EVERYTHING

Where did the client get the idea that for a $2,000 advertising investment, he should get a minimum of a dozen people spending $60,000 on his lot? Did that actually occur in the past when he advertised with someone else? If so, what did he advertise? Was he giving anything away? Or, is it possible that the client's expectation came out of thin air?

Well, it doesn't matter whether the client's thinking is logical or illogical. The thing that matters is that is what the client believes. And in the long run, **the client's perception is everything**. So you see how important it is to listen to the client, find out what his perceptions, or misperceptions are, and then educate him about how to reasonably calculate return on advertising expenditures. In other words, you must manage the client's expectations about results on your station.

By knowing what her average sale and profit margin are, we can:

- Help our client calculate return on investment and manage her expectations about advertising results on our station.
- Encounter less rate resistance.
- Encounter less added value.
- Double or triple the amount of money the client is thinking about spending with us.
- Make more local direct sales regardless of your format or programming.
- More easily convince a client to purchase a long-term contract.

WHY IGNORANCE AND MISMANAGED EXPECTATIONS CAUSE RATE RESISTANCE

Over and over I hear the same thing from sellers and managers. "How do I overcome rate resistance? I have been calling on this client for six months now and all he says is that I am too expensive. I don't know what to do with this client."

LET'S START WITH WHY RATE RESISTANCE EVER COMES UP TO BEGIN WITH

Rate resistance is a consequence of a client's lack of perceived value in you or your station. When someone is uneducated about a particular product or service, the first objection is always the price or rate. Think about it. When someone is trying to sell you something you do not completely understand, the rate or cost will always be your first line of defense. It is the first "card" you will use in your "hand" of resistance. I've got a personal example for you.

While remodeling the exterior of my house recently, my wife pointed out that both the pool and the spa needed attention badly. She had taken several bids on refurbishing our thirty-year-old swimming pool. I thought the cost was astronomical, but after comparing bids, I became okay with a general price range for the work we needed done. But I put my foot down on the spa. "Thirty-five hundred MAX is what we will pay for that spa," I told her. And, she agreed. By the way, we knew nothing about spas. We had never shopped for a new one.

So, we went spa shopping. We visited five or six reputable places. They listened to me as I told them what I wanted and they all nodded when I laid down the law on the price I was willing to pay. "Well, Paul," they said. "Sure, you can get a spa for $3,500. But it won't be the same spa you're looking at here on the showroom floor. It will be one of these over here." I wasn't impressed with what they showed me, but I was sticking to the price. "Sure, it's a working spa," they told me. "But the motors aren't really that powerful. In fact, when you turn the jets on, it might feel like somebody is peeing on you. And, if the thing breaks, who's going to fix it? The warranty's not very good."

By the time I had heard the same story five or six times, I had no problem revising my estimate for the spa. I wound up paying more than $5,000. And, I am very happy now with my purchase. When one of the motors went out, the company came by within two days and installed a brand new motor. So the question becomes, where did I come up with the number $3,500? Truthfully? I pulled it out of thin air. I did. And, I am sure you've done the same thing with some other product or service.

During the budgeting process, where do you think a lot of companies come up with the figure they'll use for advertising? Is it possible that they too, will pull a number out of the air? Remember that for most companies, the side of the marketing triangle that says advertising is always the weakest link. It is the hardest side to qualify and to quantify. It is always the most mysterious side of the marketing triangle.

So if their perception were that advertising is a crapshoot to begin with, why would they risk much on that budget item? They know far more about the product/service side of their triangle. They know far more about the sales force side. And, they know the least about the mysterious advertising side. So, which side will get the shortest end of the stick?

Educated clients buy more than uneducated clients. That is why I take every local direct client through all six of the marketing concepts, the difference between good and bad advertising, and how to calculate return on investment. I know that if my client is on the same page I am regarding the importance of advertising to the overall success of her business, she is much more likely to spend more with me, because now advertising on my station looks less like a crapshoot and more like a good, calculated risk.

When I can show a client the huge hole in a competitor's advertising and marketing strategy and explain the rules for the difference between a good and a bad spot and when I can show him how to calculate return on investment for any advertising he does, I might double or triple the amount the client thinks he can risk on my station. Rate resistance goes away. No added value even comes into the discussion. It does not make any difference whether I am number one or number twenty. And, what's wrong with that?

IT REALLY FEELS GOOD TO STOP BEATING YOUR HEAD AGAINST THE WALL

Sometimes, we get ourselves into a trap in dealing with local direct clients, who are consumed with nothing but rate. Typically, these are clients who have become spoiled over time, because every chiquita from every station in town is "educating" them with nothing more than rates and ratings. Many of these clients are now completely consumed with rate thinking and it will be very, very difficult to get them to focus on anything else. What to do?

Occasionally, it is just a good idea to give up on the contentious rate-oriented client. Fire that client, and then call on competitors.

Tell them, "So-and-so" isn't branding our listeners or viewers. That means that you have an opportunity to educate our audience now, with less competition for mind share.

When you make a sale, be sure to ask for a long-term contract. This will give you time to build a good relationship with your new client, and the annual contract your client signed will keep the wolves and chiquitas from the other stations at bay—for a while. But, after you have proven yourself to be a real resource and a good friend to your client, your rate will become secondary to your value as a consultant.

W o r k s h e e t: Explaining the Pure Logic of Buying Your Station

1. ROI calculations do so much to manage client expectations about results and double or triple advertising budgets. Yet some salespeople don't use the concept because they haven't fully absorbed the process. Are you having trouble working with the ROI formula? What part or parts of the concept are you having problems understanding? Don't just blow this off. Write down the parts you don't understand and go over the material again until the concept becomes clear to you.

2. List three reasons why it's in your best interest to discuss return on investment with your local direct clients.

3. You're asking a client to run a thirty spot per week schedule on your station. Your client owns a restaurant. The average sale at the restaurant is $50. The client's gross profit margin is 45 percent. How many new customers must your station motivate to come to the restaurant in order for your client to break even on his advertising?

CHAPTER
■■■ 16 ■■■

The Value of One New Customer

ENHANCING THE "MAGIC NUMBER"

Now, here's the icing on the cake. Explain the value of one new customer that you could bring to your client's business. What I mean is, does your client's average customer come back for more? And does your client's typical satisfied customer recommend your client to his friends, family, and co-workers?

What's the value of one new customer? An independent insurance agency says it has customers that go back three generations, from when the agency was founded. Grandparents recommended the agency to their children, and now grandchildren are buying policies from the same agency. An auto insurance premium for two average drivers runs $1,200 per year. And if a customer buys an auto policy, he's twice as likely to buy a homeowners policy from the same agency. The premium for the homeowner's policy averages $800 per year. Again, the average customer sticks with this agent for many, many years.

Automotive manufacturer Lexus said the value of one new satisfied Lexus customer is $600,000. That is, the typical Lexus customer will probably buy a second Lexus and maybe another for a spouse. He would recommend the car to friends and co-workers. In other words, although he owns no stock in the Lexus Corporation, he becomes one of their best salespeople.

CREATURES OF HABIT

People are creatures of habit, and we become evangelists about the places we love to go. If you get used to going to a particular restaurant, you're liable to visit that restaurant perhaps once a week, or at least once a quarter. If somebody asked you where you wanted to go eat, wouldn't you recommend your favorite place? You bet you would. We make free commercials for the businesses we love every time we try to talk a friend or a relative, or even a stranger on the street if she asks your opinion on a particular product or service. Heck, we don't even wait for people to ask. We seek out others to tell. "Oh, man, we ate at the best restaurant last night. I have never had a steak that good. And the dessert? Mmmmmmm! Best cheesecake I've ever tasted. You have to try it!" We are all evangelists for businesses that we love.

If you love the coffee house around the corner from where you work or live, you might visit it every single morning. If somebody suggests that you meet somewhere for breakfast, you would probably recommend your favorite little coffee house. What's the average sale at a coffee house? At least $5, if you buy something to eat as well as order a cup of coffee. So if you visited every working day, the average sale becomes $25 instead of just $5 per week, doesn't it? What's one new very loyal customer worth to the owner of a coffee house over the course of a year? $1,300! And that doesn't include referrals and recommendations the customer might make to other people.

THE VALUE OF ONE NEW CUSTOMER COULD BE HUGE

Let's say that a dentist, for example, operates on a 40 percent gross profit margin. His average sale for just a checkup and teeth cleaning could be more than $100 per visit. Most people go to the dentist at least twice per year. And what happens if you crack a tooth, or need a filling or (God forbid) need a root canal or some other procedure? How long have you been going to the same dentist? One year? Two years? Longer? How often do you visit your dentist? Twice or three times per year? Do others from your family use the same dentist? If someone moved into town and asked you to recommend a dentist, would you recommend yours? The value of one new customer to your dentist could be thousands of dollars over a few short years. How big is your total weekly audience? Doesn't it seem logical that with a good spot and a logical schedule, a percentage of your audience might be looking for a new dentist this week?

The value of one new customer to your client could be very significant. Imagine the value of one new customer if that customer wields tremendous influence over large groups of people. If this influential individual likes a particular product or service, and becomes an evangelist about it, he could drive incredible amounts of business to your client.

EDUCATE EVERY LOCAL DIRECT CLIENT

An uneducated client probably has no logical basis for the amount of money she is spending. Uneducated broadcast salespeople usually don't have any logical basis for the budget they are asking for. In fact, most broadcast salespeople just pull a number out of thin air!

Always explain Return on Investment (ROI) and impress upon the client the value of one new customer. It's very difficult to argue with this kind of logic and remember, we're doing several things in the process:

1. Eliminating rate resistance.
2. Eliminating the need for added value.
3. Closing a sale whether you're rated number one or number twenty.
4. Managing the client's expectations about results on your station.
5. Possibly doubling or tripling the amount of money your client is spending with you.
6. More easily convincing the client to purchase a long-term contract.

W o r k s h e e t: The Value of One New Customer

Enhance your client's "magic number" by asking about the value of one new customer that your station might bring to his business.

1. Calculate ROI for a high-end restaurant. Let's say the average sale is $100 and the client's gross margin of profit is 45 percent. How many new customers would you have to deliver from your station in order to justify a twenty-spot weekly schedule on your station? Armed with this information, go to a restaurant owner and ask him how often his average satisfied customer comes back in a year.

2. The value of one new long-term customer is just as important for you as it is a client. What is your average sale at your station? Multiply that times twelve months and then calculate your commission. What if you had that same customer for five years? How much money would you make?

CHAPTER
▪▪▪ 17 ▪▪▪

Selling Against Other Media

O ne of the easiest ways to prospect for new clients is by going after accounts already advertising with somebody else. Why not? Someone else has already done most of the work by convincing the client to advertise to begin with. Now all you have to do is contact that client and educate him on the benefits of using your station as well. Unfortunately, that prospecting strategy works both ways. While you're prospecting other media, it is logical to assume that other media are also prospecting you. To be more effective in your prospecting efforts and at the same time protect what you have on the air, you should know how to sell against other media. You should know the strengths and weaknesses of other media, and you should be aware of what other media are saying about radio and television's weaknesses. We'll do that in this chapter. Then we'll look at strategies to divert money local clients are spending on other media to your station. First, let's examine the strengths and weaknesses of other media.

NEWSPAPER

Die-hard newspaper clients can be tough customers. Despite recent declines in subscriptions and readership, newspapers have been around for hundreds of years and their value to many local advertisers is deeply ingrained. It's no wonder. Newspaper advertising has many perceived advantages.

- **Room to display multiple products and services.** Display ads can serve as a "laundry list," allowing advertisers to feature many items, prices, photos, and other detailed messages.
- **Tangible reference value.** It's undeniable; customers come in with newspaper coupons in their hands.
- **Literate people spend a lot of time with the newspaper.** Daily subscribers or readers are usually better educated than the population at large. And better education usually means higher income and more buying power.
- **Advertising by section.** The newspaper affords the advertiser the option of narrowing the audience by section—sports, life style, real estate, automotive, etc.
- **Easy to use.** Advertisers are comfortable writing and designing their own ads.
- **Websites.** Newspapers have been better than some other media at developing and utilizing online services for advertisers. In fact, over 40 percent of all local money spent on Internet advertising now goes to the newspaper's website.

However, newspapers are not without their Achilles heel. Among the newspaper's biggest problems are:

- **High cost, despite declining readership.** Newspaper subscriptions are down nationwide. There is no question about that. But in spite of the declining circulation numbers, newspapers are still getting annual rate increases. Figure that one out. Compare your total weekly CUME audience to the newspaper's biggest number, weekly READERSHIP. Is it possible that your radio or tv station out-CUMEs their audience? What does a full-page ad cost in your town's paper? With a full-page ad, does your client *own* that day in the paper? No. There are too many other pages. If the client spent the same amount of money on your station that she spends on a full-page newspaper ad, could she *own* your station for a day, or at least a program or two on your station in a day? Typically, the answer is yes.

- **Lack of young audience.** Newspaper's most rapid decline in circulation is in the Adult 18–34 demographic. This audience spends a lot of consumer dollars. But you can't reach them effectively with newspaper. Broadcast audiences are more diverse, by program or format. Younger people may not be reading the newspaper, but they do spend a lot of time with radio and television.

- **Passive medium.** The newspaper doesn't deliver a message at all unless you pick it up and turn the pages. Until then it says nothing. It just sits there on the table. Even if you pick up a paper and thumb through it, the ads are silent. They just sit there, emotionless in mostly black and white. Broadcast commercials are not passive. They are active. Radio and television commercials jump right out and talk to you.

- **Little if any competitive protection.** Newspapers don't offer competitive protection. That is, they'll run competitor's ads right next to each other. Broadcast stations typically try to offer competitive protection whenever possible.

- **Clutter.** Many newspapers are 75 percent advertising. Small ads get lost in the clutter.

YELLOW PAGES

Like I said, all media are good. One of the strongest competitors for broadcast dollars continues to be the Yellow Pages. True, in many markets the Yellow Pages may now have a competitor. But let's face it, the Yellow Pages (all together) takes a big chunk of money out of virtually every market. And many businesses feel that they absolutely must have an ad in the Book. Here are some of the strengths of the Yellow Pages:

- People turn to the Yellow Pages when they are **ready to buy**.
- Like newspapers, Yellow Pages ads can **display multiple products and services**.
- Yellow Pages can place ads for one client in **several different product/service categories**.
- **Couponing.** Like the newspaper, Yellow Page customers can find coupons they can bring directly to the advertiser.
- **Ubiquitous.** Yellow Pages are everywhere. And usually right next to the telephone.

Like newspaper, Yellow Page advertising does have its drawbacks. Here are some examples.

- **High cost.** Yellow Pages advertising can be very expensive, particularly when the advertiser is running full-page color ads in several product/service categories. And if you dispute your bill, your phone could be cut off.
- **You can't change the copy.** The advertiser is stuck with the same copy for a year. That's a long time, especially if the advertiser has something new and more competitive he'd like to say. And what if there's a mistake in the ad? Too bad. You live with it for a year. With broadcast you can change an ad very quickly.
- **Passive medium.** Again, a Yellow Pages ad doesn't say anything until you pick it up and turn the pages. Up to that point the book sits in a drawer or under piles of mail.
- **Absolutely no competitive protection.** When you shop the Yellow Pages, you shop all of a client's competitors too.
- **The biggest ads are in the front of the product/service category.** Sounds nice, until you think about it. "When you buy a full page ad in our Yellow Pages, we'll put your ad right in the front of the section!" Fine, except most people thumb through the Yellow Pages from back to front. Try it yourself. Pick up the phone book and look at the way you actually handle it to get to the pawnbrokers section. That means that in

reality, customers will see the smaller ads before they get to the big, expensive ones in the front of the section.

- **Clutter.** The Yellow Pages is virtually all ads. For small businesses, it's becoming very expensive to compete in the phone book, particularly if you need multiple listings. For example, if you're in the heating and air conditioning business, you'll need an ad in heating and another in air conditioning. If you're in the appliance business, you'd need listings in refrigerators, stoves, washing machines, etc.

- **Too many books.** Clients in many markets are being courted by multiple "Yellow Pages" books. Which book (or books) should the client buy?

- **The Internet.** Many younger people use the Internet for searching out businesses. And there are many different Internet "Yellow Pages." Older people may have trouble with the Yellow Pages as well. In big cities the books are big and the older you get, the harder it is to read the numbers.

CABLE

The cable industry has made huge progress in recent years, and most homes now subscribe to either a cable or a satellite system. Many local businesses sense that when they buy cable, they're getting broadcast tv at radio station rates. Cable companies are better organized and have better salespeople than they had just a decade ago, many making the switch from radio and broadcast tv. But with respect to all of the other sources of revenue available to the cable company, advertising is still pretty low on the totem pole. Other more profitable cable revenue sources include:

- Cable subscription
- Broadband Internet subscription
- Entertainment and sports pay-per-view
- Telephone service

Still, cable is making inroads with local direct clients, and it is taking business away from local radio and television stations. Television executives do their best to convince clients that broadcast television and cable are two different things but many local advertisers perceive very little difference between cable and terrestrial television. Cable and broadcast television now come into most homes through the same box and cable looks just like television. People in their forties and older remember a time when there were only four (or fewer) choices when it came to watching television, the ABC, CBS, NBC, and PBS affiliate stations. Today, of course, there are hundreds of stations available through cable and there are always more on the way. Let's discuss the strengths of cable as an advertising medium.

- **Frequency.** Because cable stations have fractions of the audience size of a broadcast television station or a radio station, prices are very low. Advertisers can therefore afford to buy more spots on cable.
- **Cost.** Cable account executives can pitch cable as "television without the high cost" or "radio with video."
- **Targeting by network.** Cable advertisers can "narrow-cast" their messages to targeted groups, like the food channel for women or the golf channel for men.
- **Reach.** The cable advertising executive can claim her company can offer a higher reach, like a broadcast station, when local clients buy a mix of cable channels.
- **Targeting by geography.** Some cable companies claim they can make a local direct client's advertising much more efficient because he can choose to purchase only in neighborhoods close to his business.
- **Cable block.** Some cable companies can arrange for a client's commercial to run at about the same time on multiple channels. So no matter what channel the viewer tunes in, she's likely to see the same commercial within five minutes or so.

Like all media, cable advertising has its share of weaknesses.

- **No reach.** Cable generates very low audience figures when compared to broadcast. Cable salespeople might claim that they have a large reach number. For example, let's say they claim they have 200,000 subscribers. But not all of those 200,000 are ever tuned in to the same channel at the same time. The largest cable audience may be equal to the smallest broadcast audience.

- **Deceptive interpretation of research.** A cable company might claim that because 80 percent of the market is wired to cable, they have an 80 percent penetration in that market. What the research really means is they have the capacity to reach 80 percent, but 100 percent of that 80 percent do not subscribe to cable. Cable may claim that it has a more affluent and better educated audience than a broadcast station. But that also means that cable fails to reach thousands of people who can't afford cable subscription but still spend money on other products and services.

- **Small daytime audience.** Cable's daytime numbers are very low. Most people don't start watching cable until 6 PM or later.

- **Reaches tight niche audiences and misses potential customers outside that niche.** Cable's narrow-cast advantage turns into a disadvantage when you consider that because of a particular channel's lack of broad appeal, fewer people in a household are likely to be watching when the set is tuned to that channel. Generally speaking, men don't like the cooking channel, and they won't watch. Women don't like the golf channel, and they won't watch.

DIRECT MAIL

You might think of it as junk mail, but many advertisers see direct mail as a gold mine. Despite rising postal costs, direct mail is still a favorite advertising medium for many businesses. Direct mail houses have access to much better mailing lists than they had just a few years ago, and they have developed faster and far more efficient processes for printing, stuffing, and sorting mail. Here is what some local direct clients like about direct mail:

- **Targeted.** The most effective direct mail comes addressed to you for a reason. Because of purchases you have made in the past or because of the location of your home or business or because of a particular interest you have, you fit a specific profile. Part of the cost of direct mail is the advertiser's access to a mailing list that contains addresses for a very specific group of people.
- **Personal.** Most direct mail arrives with the targeted person's name on the envelope. Advertising in most other media cannot address you specifically by name and precise location.
- **Measurable.** Direct mailers can easily track response through coupon redemption, return mail, and telephone callback.
- **Reach.** Direct mail could potentially reach every household the advertiser desires.

Direct mail also has many drawbacks.

- **Growing cost.** Everything about direct mail is getting more expensive. Postage rates, paper costs, processing fees, printing and production costs, and access to more targeted mailing lists are all getting more and more expensive.
- **Low response rate.** Most direct mail gets thrown away unopened.
- **Public perception.** Most people perceive direct mail as "junk mail."
- **Outdated or inaccurate mailing lists.** Direct mail is expensive and if the mailing list the advertiser purchases isn't current or if the data isn't accurate for the advertiser's target, he's throwing away money.

OUTDOOR BILLBOARDS

Like junk mail, consumers generally hate billboards, but many advertisers love them, especially if the billboard is geographically near the client's business. Nothing works better if you're driving and you are sleepy or hungry than a billboard promising food or a room for the night and huge letters that say, "NEXT EXIT." Unfortunately, many local advertisers waste money on billboard advertising because they don't know what they are doing. For example, they try to cram too much information on one board that no people could possibly read as they drive past at 70 miles per hour. Most experts agree that in order to be effective, the maximum number of words on a billboard should be no more than seven. Here are some of the advantages to using outdoor:

- **High reach.** Highway billboards are passed by thousands of cars per day.
- **Frequency.** Billboards typically stay up for at least a month so people see them frequently.
- **Low cost.** In spite of the fact that there is typically a waiting list for prime locations, the billboard industry has kept the cost per thousand down below that of other media.
- **Directional/Geographic.** Advertisers can place them in specific geographical areas and in specific directions. "Next Exit" is a powerful statement.
- **On 24 hours a day.** They can't be turned off. A bright billboard is difficult not to notice.

Outdoor disadvantages:

- **No targeting.** Everybody sees them as they drive by so there is no way to skew demographically.
- **Limited information, limited exposure.** Again, seven words maximum and people only have a few seconds to see them.

- **Blight on the landscape.** Many people hate them and communities have reduced their numbers and locations. Legislation has reduced billboard inventory.

- **Weather.** Storms can tear them up or limit consumer exposure.

- **You can't change the copy.** Like Yellow Pages ads, billboards are inflexible if you need to change copy.

THE INTERNET

For local direct clients, the Internet is now moving beyond just putting up a boring website. It's moving beyond ineffective banner ads. In fact, Internet advertising is evolving into a lucrative guaranteed ROI machine for some savvy local direct clients. Broadcast account executives are complaining that local direct clients are using traditional broadcast dollars to develop their Internet strategy, and financial evidence tells us that more broadcast money is moving to the Internet. The Internet "elephant in the room" can no longer be ignored as just a minor irritant to the broadcast community. National websites like myspace.com, craigslist.com, and others have huge local and regional communities. With Search Engine Optimization (SEO) and Cost-Per-Click (CPC) advertising, an advertiser can choose "key words" to attract web-browsing consumers. The advertiser only pays when a consumer opens his or her page. Unfortunately, this can lead to "click fraud," a growing scam where businesses may be charged for fraudulent clickthroughs. Nonetheless, Internet advertising is on the verge of becoming a mainstream medium. If you doubt this, look at the increasing budgets newspapers, Yellow Pages, and broadcast stations are using to beef up their websites. Despite all of the positive news about online advertising, the Internet still has its share of problems for local direct businesses. First, let's look at some Internet advantages for local direct clients.

- **Tracking.** Within minutes a client can tell whether his or her ad is working. A business can literally track "cradle to purchase."

- **Qualified traffic.** The Internet attracts more educated consumers who are ready to buy.

- **Efficiency.** Businesses advertising on the Internet pay only for the clickthroughs to their websites.

- **Education.** A good website can go into significant detail about a client's business, educating potential customers about the client's strengths and product/service category.

- **People are spending more time on local websites.** City Search, myspace.com, Craig's List, and other national websites have local links. This means that a local carpet installer could have better local Internet visibility.

And here are some Internet advertising warts for local direct clients:

- **Internet advertising may not be appropriate for all businesses.** If you don't have an online store, then the only appropriate Internet expenditure might be a website only, to teach locals who you are, what you do, and how to get in touch with you.

- **Security concerns.** Big national and international Internet sites have the financial resources to provide better security. A local business might not have the money to properly protect a client's confidential data from hackers. Additionally, some consumers are still paranoid about doing business online.

- **Requires a level of sophistication.** Many potential consumers still do not have Internet access. Out of those who do, a great percentage still use a slow dial-up modem. And many local direct clients don't understand how technically involved it can be to compete with "key words," much less afford the financial investment it would entail. On a Google search, the local client may wind up very low on the totem pole.

- **Dotcom clutter causes ignored Internet advertising.** There are now literally billions of websites. People have trouble even remembering popular Internet addresses. Small businesses find themselves lost in the clutter.

- **Pay per click is getting more expensive.** In just a year or two, cost-per-click costs have tripled.

- **Accountability problems.** Unlike newspapers, magazines, and broadcast media, search engine advertising is not independently audited. This leads to problems like click fraud, where businesses can be billed for fraudulent traffic clicked through to an e-commerce site. Businesses pay Google, for example, for each valid click that brings Internet users to a business website. Scam artists send bogus clicks to a business website, inflating the amount of money that business would have to pay for clickthroughs from a hyperlink. Independent Internet auditors say as much as $400 out of every $1,000 that a business pays to Google may be due to click fraud. Google is currently fighting class action lawsuits that stem from click fraud allegations.

When broadcast salespeople learn the pluses and minuses of competitive media, we can talk to clients intelligently about all of their media choices. Remember that all media are good and it could be counterproductive to try to convince, for example, a die-hard newspaper user that radio or television is a better medium than the paper. Point out that media mixes are usually a good idea, and tell your client how broadcast strengths can help overcome some of the weaknesses in his or her other media. For example, you could single out the clutter factor that a client experiences when he uses newspaper and then recommend that on radio and television you could "showcase" the newspaper ad by mentioning in the spot, "be sure and look at our newspaper ad in tomorrow's sports section. It's the one with the picture of the sumo wrestler."

The same strategy works with direct mail. "Mr. Client, we could showcase your mailer from all of the homeowner's other mailbox clutter by reminding people in our commercials to be sure and look for your specific piece. We could even say, 'don't throw away the mail you get from John's Pizza because if you do, you're throwing away about $15 worth of discounts.'"

With the 12 billion websites out there, it's a no-brainer that your client should use broadcast advertising to teach potential customers about his or her website and refer listeners and viewers to his or her page. Your station may have a website that you could use to help move traffic to your client's page.

Remind cable advertisers that although cable looks like television, the audience on any particular cable station is very, very small. Its biggest audience may be smaller than your smallest audience. Tell the client that his or her cable choice probably only caters to a small niche. The client should use your station to make sure all bases are covered in your market, then pepper cheap cable spots in appropriate niche stations. If you work in television, tell your client that you have a better in-house production department that can create more effective commercials.

Now let's take a look at broadcast's strengths as well as some broadcast weaknesses that reps from other media may be using to take dollars away from your station.

RADIO

Radio is still a favorite advertising medium for local direct clients, and it has been since the 1930s. Clients can "narrow-cast" on radio; that is, they can pick and choose among many different formats to reach specific demographic groups. Over 95 percent of all Americans still listen to the radio every week. Most people listen to the radio in their cars. A radio commercial may be the last advertisement a consumer is exposed to before he parks his car and makes a buying decision. For all of radio's in-car advantages, in-home listening for radio is generally low.

Because radio spots don't cost a lot of money, advertisers can afford more frequency, which means they can afford to run more ads. The tradeoff for radio's higher frequency potential is its potential lack of reach. Because of the high number of radio stations in a given area, the radio audience is split many ways. So in order to achieve a high reach, the advertiser would have to buy more stations and sacrifice radio's low cost incentive in the process.

Radio stations can broadcast live and/or endorsements. A product or service endorsed by a listener's favorite personality lends credibility to that business. In many cases, a listener will walk into a business and tell someone that the personality recommended it. Clients can also tie in to station promotional activities that give their businesses extra exposure.

Radio production is inexpensive and even free to local clients in most cases. Due to lack of graphics and video, radio spots can be produced or changed very quickly.

Here are some of the things advertisers like about radio:

- **High frequency.** Low cost means you can buy more spots.
- **Emotion.** A well written and produced radio commercial can evoke an emotional response in the listener.
- **Promotions.** Clients may buy live or endorsed commercials. Clients may also tie in with other clients during promotional events.
- **In-car.** Radio still dominates in-car advertising.
- **Competitive protection.** Radio stations try to avoid running commercials from clients from the same product/service category back to back or during the same quarter hour.
- **Level playing field.** The largest client on a station can only run sixty seconds or less. A smaller advertiser can also run sixty seconds. The largest advertiser on a station can only run about a spot an hour. A small client might also own a spot an hour, for a day.
- **Immediacy.** A client can change copy quickly, sometimes within one hour.

Here are some of the problems other media salespeople like to point out to clients about radio and ways you can respond.

- **Objection:** Low in-home listening—people listen to radio only in their cars. Hardly anybody listens at home.

- **Response:** This is not true. What about people who wake up to their alarm clock radios and then listen as they're preparing for work and school? And what about at-work listening? Many people listen to the radio all day while they're working. Yes, radio dominates in-car advertising. What's wrong with that? And at the same time we reach people at home and at work.

- **Objection:** Radio commercials are not tangible. You can't hold the ad in your hand and carry it into the store like you can with newspaper.

- **Response:** Couponing on radio only fails when there is very little in it for the listener. If you really want to test radio, give away something substantial, like 42-inch flat-screen plasma televisions, instead of just 5 percent off your regular price. I guarantee you'll be inundated with radio listeners who hear your commercial and respond within minutes. Sound ridiculous? Not really, Mr. Client. What you're really saying is that somewhere between a 5 percent discount and a flat-screen television would be a good test for our listeners. Use radio and newspaper together. Let us showcase your newspaper ad in our radio copy. That will help your newspaper ad stand out from all of the clutter in the paper. Or better yet, use spot advertising to drive traffic to your store's Internet site. There customers could print out coupons. Or, advertise on our website and we'll drive traffic to your site.

- **Objection:** Audio only—limited information means no videos, pictures, or other visuals. Radio is limited to audio and "theater of the mind."

- **Response:** Did you say limited to theater of the mind? There is no limit. Radio can inexpensively paint a limitless supply of mental images in listener's mind. It may now be possible that your station's website could play your client's videos, even infomercials.

- **Objection:** Low reach—radio audiences are fragmented, which means smaller audiences for each station.

- **Response:** Yes, and at the same time our rates are lower so you can afford to reach out to our listeners multiple times.

- **Objection:** Too many stations—like a Chinese menu, most communities have so many stations with so many different formats that buying radio can appear confusing or complicated.

- **Response:** It's not that complicated, Ms. Advertiser. You are trying to reach a specific demographic group. In this market that limits your options to stations.

- **Objection:** Increasingly fragmented audience—people are listening to other devices like MP3 players, satellite radio, and compact discs in their cars.

- **Response:** Since eight-track tape players came on the scene, people have had access to other media in the car. Even now there is plenty of evidence that free radio is still by far the dominant medium in the car.

BROADCAST TELEVISION

Since its inception in the 1950s, television has become one of the most effective advertising vehicles in history. Despite television's higher cost (both production cost and spot cost), advertisers can't seem to buy enough of it. Twenty-six cents out of every dollar spent in advertising still winds up on television.

Television advertisers enjoy the best of three worlds: sight, sound, and motion. When used correctly, television can be a highly effective medium because it takes advantage of a basic human instinct. Like cats (another predator with eyes centered on the front of the face), people preternaturally like to watch things move. Television plays right into that basic human instinct.

Broadcast television generally offers a very high reach potential. That is, many people are likely to be watching a broadcast television program at any given time, especially in prime time. And advertisers (national, regional, and local) will pay premium rates to reach these larger audiences.

Many businesses perceive that television advertising is more glamorous than other media, that somehow television is a more prestigious advertising vehicle than say, radio, billboard, or direct mail. Advertising agencies may recommend television to their clients because with higher rates and more expensive schedule costs, the agency's commission is higher. Agencies also make big bucks from television spot production.

Television's higher cost presents a problem for some advertisers. That is, television spots may be so expensive to buy that you can't afford to run your commercials as frequently as you'd like. So when buying television, there is always a tradeoff. You're buying a large audience (reach), but you can't afford to advertise as often (frequency). Compromising lower frequency for higher reach is the gamble you take with broadcast tv, so the commercials that you air had better be efficient and effective.

Here are some of the reasons local advertisers like broadcast television:

- **Sight, sound, and motion.** Local direct clients can use sound along with photos, animation, graphics, and video.

- **High reach.** Broadcast television stations have massive CUME audiences, usually bigger than the newspaper's readership number.

- **Formatted by program.** One television station could reach many demographic groups with an array of different program choices.

- **Level playing field.** The biggest advertiser on a station can only run thirty seconds or less. A small advertiser can also run a thirty-second ad. The largest client on a television station might run two spots in a program. A smaller advertiser could also own two spots in a television program.

- **Prestige.** Many clients perceive that advertising on television represents the pinnacle of success. Some advertisers stroke their egos by appearing in their own commercials.

- **In-home advantage.** Viewers invite commercials into their homes.

Here is what competitive media may be saying about broadcast television and how you might respond:

- **Objection:** Commercial time on broadcast television is expensive—television's cost per spot is much higher than with radio or cable.

- **Response:** You get what you pay for. If we reach a significantly larger audience than other media, we deserve to be paid for it.

- **Objection:** High-cost production—because of all of the elements involved video, graphics, and sound, television commercials generally cost more to produce.

- **Response:** This is no longer necessarily true. With the advances we've made technologically, it is now possible at many television stations to make agency-quality commercials for a fraction of the cost.

- **Objection:** Long production lead time—due to the tedious nature of television spot production and a shortage of production facilities, it can take a while to produce a new spot.

- **Response:** In the past this may have been the case. But again with modern production facilities, we're able to work much faster than before.

- **Objection:** No frequency—because of television's higher cost per spot it's difficult for a local business to buy a lot of television.

- **Response:** That depends on a number of factors, including how and when you buy us. Let's work out an ROI analysis and see whether you can afford not to use us.

- **Objection:** Almost all viewing is done at home—people don't usually watch television at work or in their cars.

- **Response:** This may be true, but don't discount the time people spend in front of their televisions at home. Hours upon hours at a time in many cases. Other media still don't compete when it comes to time spent watching television at home.

- **Objection:** Increasingly fragmented home audience—the proliferation of competitive devices like video games, DVD players, and computers is affecting the number of hours that people watch television.

- **Response:** We've had competitive media in homes since the VCRs and Atari game machines first came along. Before that we had other competitors like Monopoly and card games. Television viewing was then and still is today number one in the home.

- **Objection:** Digital video recorders allow commercial zapping—TiVo and other DVRs are becoming commonplace in most homes.

- **Response:** Research also shows that since the inception of DVRs, people are actually watching more television than they did before. Clever television commercials can cause people to stop fast-forward and watch.

As you can see, there are many ways to take advantage of the "holes" in other media and at the same time defend broadcast from attacks by other media. The most effective and least-used strategy for getting dollars from other media is to go after products and services that are completely overrepresented on other media and underrepresented on yours.

For example, most tire stores advertise in print, the newspapers, and the Yellow Pages. Smart broadcast sellers cull one client from the herd and say, "Look, the Yellow Pages/newspaper is a good medium. That is, it's a big lake with lots of fish in it. I also represent a big lake with lots of fish. But Mr. Tire Man, in your particular product/service category, wouldn't you agree that the newspaper/Yellow Pages is being a little overfished? When somebody comes to the newspaper/Yellow Pages, they're shopping all of your competitors. Every single one of you has a line in the water when you use the newspaper/Yellow Pages. But look at our nice lake. We have thousands of consumers who will need tires sooner or later and we don't have one single tire dealer fishing on our lake. You'd practically have a monopoly here on our lake."

Use your strengths against other media's weaknesses and get more local direct advertisers. It may take time to whittle down a die-hard newspaper or Yellow Pages user, so do it in stages. Over time give your client ammunition she can use against her reps from other media. Help the client chisel out a budget for you by cutting back on her buys on other media.

W o r k s h e e t: Selling Against Other Media

1. Name three weaknesses for each medium.
   - **Newspaper**
     1. _____
     2. _____
     3. _____
   - **Yellow Pages**
     1. _____
     2. _____
     3. _____
   - **Cable**
     1. _____
     2. _____
     3. _____
   - **Direct Mail**
     1. _____
     2. _____
     3. _____
   - **Outdoor**
     1. _____
     2. _____
     3. _____
   - **Internet**
     1. _____
     2. _____
     3. _____

2. Discuss your medium's strengths.

CHAPTER

■■■ 18 ■■■

Why a Local Broadcast Client Should Own Your Station

Now that you understand the principles of ROI and how to explain them to your clients, let's discuss what type of schedules you should be selling, and why you should pitch higher frequency. We in the broadcast sales business have gotten ourselves into a deep rut when it comes to what clients pay us for schedules on our stations. Many local clients don't perceive value with radio and television the same way they do with Yellow Pages and print. Subsequently, we expect and we get just a pittance of the percentage of the budget that the print medium routinely gets.

For example, many local direct clients don't have a problem buying big ads in the newspaper, but they have a huge problem justifying your little piddly $3,500 monthly schedule. How did this happen? Do clients simply pay us less because "that's the way we've always done it"? That's not logical.

Isn't it possible that your big 12+ CUME number comes close or exceeds the newspaper's weekly readership number? Even if your CUME doesn't approach the newspaper's readership figure (generally circulation times 2.3 = readership), compare the efficiency factor. Let's say that the newspaper has a weekly readership of 400,000. Your station reaches 40,000 different people in a week. The newspaper gets $10,000 for a full-page ad. Running fifteen spots in a day (at $40.00 per spot) on your station would cost only, say, $600.

The paper may have ten times your weekly audience but they're asking for and getting much more than ten times your cost for a day's advertising. And even with a full-page ad in the paper, the client doesn't own the day in newspaper. There are just too many pages. Priced as you are, your station would probably do a much more efficient and effective job, because if you run a spot an hour for a day on a broadcast station, you own that station for that day.

Most clients aren't giving away Rolex watches or flat-screen televisions to the first 100,000 people who walk into their stores today. In fact, most clients aren't giving away anything when they advertise. So I believe in frequency. Cast good bait and cast it often enough so that people who are *on* for that product or service have a chance to see or hear the bait.

It's a shame that we see so many businesses these days trying to sell "Cadillac" products and services with "Festiva"-sized advertising budgets. When a client tells you that he "tried it (radio or television) once and it didn't work," it is likely that he didn't buy the medium correctly. Especially now, with the average consumer being exposed to a minimum of 5,000 commercial impressions per day, local businesses must embrace the concept of frequency when they advertise. As media professionals, we must advise our clients to own a day or own a daypart or own a program on a broadcast station.

It makes logical sense for businesses to own real estate on your station. You should have already made a good case for that with your client. Remind her that it is critical to maintain a good and constant presence on your station for several important reasons.

1. To reach audience members who are *on* right now for what she is selling.

2. To begin the branding process with the rest of your audience. Remind the client that yes, logically and statistically, a percentage of your listeners or viewers are *on* right now for her product or service (provided your demographic matches her and provided she doesn't have marketing problems) but a greater percentage of your audience might come *on* at some point in the future. Therefore, it is necessary to

brand those people, so that when they do come *on*, they might consider your client when they shop, instead of going straight to a competitor.

3. As insurance against bad word of mouth. Radio and television advertising is controlled word of mouth.

So, it is logical that your client should own real estate on your station and also maintain a constant presence on your station. Mention selling long term, not cheap, patchy ROS (Run-of-Station).

DON'T WATER IT DOWN

Most ROS schedules are a product of ignorance. Look at it this way, most radio and television stations run about a thousand spots a week. So running a fifteen-spot ROS schedule through a week would be terrible coverage. Imagine that one spot on your station equaled about a liter. If you ran that fifteen-spot Run-of-Station (ROS) schedule on your station, that would be like pouring a bottle of fine champagne into 300 gallons of water! You wouldn't taste very much champagne, would you?

Agencies buy ROS because it *looks* efficient on a computer report. However, agencies are not in the business of buying results for their clients. They are only interested in reaching media efficiency goals. As far as I'm concerned, efficiency and results for a client are two completely different things. I'm certainly more interested in helping my client achieve measurable results. I do this by calculating ROI, creating a good, compelling spot, and then running that commercial enough times to reach new customers, give old customers reasons to come back, and educate future customers. The client tracks advertising progress by measuring weekly and monthly revenues against the same periods from the previous year. Clients might not always be able to determine the precise cause of a surge in business, but they can always measure the effect—increased revenues.

OWN A PROGRAM OR DAYPART

Running ten or fifteen spots per day or owning a daypart like morning drive or midday or overnight is the best way to use radio. Instead of running twenty-one spots throughout a week—Monday–Saturday, for example—you might own Tuesday and Wednesday, especially if the client has a service-oriented business and doesn't need Thursdays and Fridays.

Run ten or more spots per day, if you can. If you really want your client to cut through the crap-o-sphere, owning a spot an hour per day or running two spots in a nightly newscast or another program is the logical and correct way to buy television. It's the right thing to do, and it's good for both you and your client. And, it certainly makes more logical sense than running a diluted ROS schedule, like some of the computer reports recommend. That's why broadcast stations hire people, rather than totally rely on computer-generated reports. The reports might indicate that a thin ROS spot schedule is efficient, but logic tells us that a thin schedule is less likely to generate results for your client.

KING FOR A DAY WITH A PUTTER

I tell clients that all media are good, but broadcast has some scheduling advantages that you just can't get in print. If you've ever played golf, maybe you might have noticed that although experienced golfers might play a great long game, they blow it on putting. Even inexperienced players accidentally sink a forty-foot putt that would be very challenging for a professional golfer. So in golfing, putting is the great equalizer. In broadcasting, time is the great equalizer.

If you buy an ad in the newspaper, the paper might run your ad right next to a very large competitor's ad. Your competitor looks great. Your client looks like a shrimp. But with broadcast you can be king for a day. A smaller advertiser can buy the same length of spot as the largest advertiser. Wal-Mart can only buy sixty seconds or less when it purchases spots on your radio station. And, a small boutique can also buy a sixty-second spot. The biggest advertiser on your television station can only buy thirty seconds or less. And, your smallest advertiser can also only purchase thirty seconds or less. So, time is the great equalizer in broadcast advertising.

Further, Wal-Mart can only run a spot per hour on your radio station before your program director becomes very irritated. A smaller advertiser could also own a spot an hour for a day. The biggest advertiser on your TV station usually runs no more than two to three commercials per program. And, a small advertiser could also run two or three commercials in a program. Time is the great equalizer in broadcast, just like putting is the great equalizer in the game of golf. Educate print advertisers about this broadcast advantage. You might also point out that it's difficult to control when people read print. If a product or service is time sensitive for example, a restaurant serving lunch or dinner—it would be more logical to own specific times of day on a radio or television station and increase the chances of catching listeners or viewers while they are "hungry" for that product or service. Time makes broadcast a level playing field.

DON'T MAKE RATES LOOK COMPLICATED AND CONFUSING

A vast majority of local direct clients have the perception that broadcast advertising is confusing, complicated, and expensive. Gee, I wonder why. If I go to the store and look for a price on an item, I can find it immediately. But that's not the way we work in broadcast. Here's a scenario.

Client: "Well, how much does it cost to buy your station?"
Broadcast Chiquita: "Well, that depends."
Client: "Depends on what?"

Broadcast Chiquita: "Well, that depends on whether you're buying mornings, middays, afternoons, nights, early fringe, prime, news, etc."

Client: "What if I bought mornings? How much would that cost?"

Broadcast Chiquita: "Well, that depends."

Client: "Depends on what?"

Broadcast Chiquita: "Well, we're on Grid 2 on Mondays. But on Tuesdays we go to Grid 3. But that's only for now because we're sold out. Wednesday through Fridays we're on Grid 4. But on Saturdays we're on Grid 3 and on Sundays, we're only on Grid 1."

Client: "Whew! Well, let me think about it."

Broadcast Chiquita: "Okay, then I'll leave you our rate card and some computer reports and a few of our special packages. But remember that near the end of the month, the grids might have to change."

It's ridiculous. Why do we make broadcast look so hard to buy? Here's a logical idea; price your station by the day. Make it as easy as possible. Estimate the total cost of running say, ten spots in one day. If your average spot rate in a day were, for example, $100, then you could tell a client that to use your station correctly would cost about $1,000 a day. Most clients don't even flinch when you tell them this. Do you know why? Because they are used to hearing a similar daily ad cost from the newspaper.

WRAPPING IT UP

Use the analogy of one bottle of champagne to 300 gallons of water to explain the logic of *owning it* to your client. Just say that diluting a radio or television campaign does not make logical sense. Own a day or a daypart or a program.

MOST LOCAL DIRECT CLIENTS ARE ALLERGIC TO RATINGS INFORMATION

Heck, most of us in the business don't understand ratings well enough to explain them in language that most local direct clients would understand. I recently had a conversation with the owner of an advertising agency. During the course of our conversation, it dawned on me that he didn't fully understand what a Gross Rating Point was. He had it all wrong. Incredible! He'd been buying radio and television schedules for years, beating up on all of his media reps and he didn't even know what he was doing.

Stop giving ratings reports and complicated rate cards to local direct clients. Instead of spending all of your time sitting at the computer chunking out efficiency reports, get out on the street and start preaching the idea of "owning" real estate. Own a day, own a daypart, own a program on our station.

Recommend it to your clients. It's the right thing to do, and it is much more logical than pitching and having to explain some goofy ROS schedule that probably won't work. Clients appreciate logical and easy-to-understand thinking and they want results.

W o r k s h e e t: Why a Local Broadcast Client Should Own Your Station

I believe in **frequency** when we run schedules. Own a **day** or own a **daypart** or own a **program** on your station, but by gosh, own it.

1. Generally speaking, describe the average or typical schedule you seem to sell the most. Briefly explain your logic.

2. Based on what we've studied in this chapter, express what changes, if any, you would make in the way you propose schedules to local direct clients.

PART
IV

Broadcast Sales Mechanics:
How to Make Your Job Easier

CHAPTER

■■■ **19** ■■■

Creating Concise and Customized Marketing and Advertising Proposals

This section will teach you a way to develop a one-sheet proposal called an SOS. What is an SOS proposal? Essentially, it's a simple, customized marketing and advertising proposal that looks like a business plan. Keep reading and I'll teach you how to write one. First, here's why you should stop winging it on something as important as a proposal and immediately begin using a structured proposal.

NO PROPOSAL? BAD IDEA

I ran into a television salesperson I hadn't seen in a while. He was excited about a second meeting with a new client in the air conditioning and heating business. I asked him what he was proposing to the client, and he spouted off several ideas. I asked him if he had a written version for the client and he said, "No, I'll just wing it." The salesperson said goodbye and ran off to his appointment.

The next time I saw the salesperson, I asked how his meeting went with the air conditioning client. He said, "Okay, but I didn't close him. He told me he tried television before, and it didn't work, but that I could send him more information in the mail. So I guess I'll mail him some stuff." Sound familiar?

Not good. The account exec had an appointment but no game plan. He wasted his time and the client's time, and he did nothing to change the client's perception that broadcast advertising is at best a crapshoot. At this point the client probably thinks the salesperson is just another chiquita. Your time is your greatest asset. Use it wisely.

COMPLICATED PROPOSALS ARE CONFUSING

Nearly every week a local direct client shows me a written proposal from a broadcast station. The client and I are always amazed at how impersonal, complicated, and totally off-the-mark most of these proposals can be. In nearly every case the only custom element of the proposal is the cover sheet. Most of these proposals contain computer-generated sheets referring to confusing concepts like frequency and AQH. I've seen proposals that were over twenty pages thick! Most contain graphs, charts, rate cards, and signal maps. But seldom do they ever contain an original idea on how the client would benefit from using the station. Many of these proposals are nothing more than standard media kits. And shamefully, most broadcast proposals are nothing more than low-rate ROS packages.

These multipage proposals often do more to scare, intimidate, and confuse a client than anything else. Seldom are they ever thoroughly read. If they're not thrown away immediately, then they will sit in a filing cabinet for a year. Eventually, they'll be thrown away without a second glance, or they'll be given away, possibly to a savvy competitor. Remember that we're trying to convince local direct clients that advertising with us is a logical and easy thing to do. So, why would we make the proposal look so complicated?

ELEMENTS OF A GOOD PROPOSAL

Like I said, the SOS proposal method is essentially a concise advertising **business plan**. Here are the elements:

SITUATION: A brief overview on how you interpret the client's specific marketing and advertising challenges based on information you've gotten directly from your first meeting with the client. Don't just regurgitate the history of the client's business. He already knows that. Instead, use "situation" to define a specific problem the client might be having with competitors or with branding or visibility. Maybe the client is advertising in a medium that's too cluttered with competitors that he can't break through.

OBJECTIVE: A brief description of what you and your station specifically hope to accomplish based on the situation described above. Your objective would include your desire to help your client to break through advertising clutter by making her advertising identifiably different from that of her competitors. You would also include a return-on-investment calculation for the number of listeners or viewers your campaign might generate based on your client's average sale and gross profit margin. Combining this information with your station's total CUME audience and your average rate, you come up with a reasonable number of paying customers that you'd have to effectively reach in order to reach a breakeven point for your client's advertising expenditure. The point here is to try to come up with a calculated goal that both you and your client think is reasonable and attainable.

STRATEGY: A concise strategy on how you propose to accomplish your objective. You would focus on your creative and scheduling strategies and specifically on how your plan would benefit your client in language that she could easily understand. Your cost would be included here as well, but not in such a way that it leaps off of the page. Although the cost of a schedule is usually the most negative item in your proposal, I've actually seen proposals where the price was the biggest and boldest font on the page. You don't want the client focusing on the cost of the schedule. You want the client to focus on the benefits. It makes logical sense to make your cost as small as possible by literally putting it in a smaller font. Instead of showing the total cost of your schedule, break it down and show it by day, for however many ("X") number of days per week. Or, "X" weeks per year. Let the client do the math.

GREAT REASONS TO USE
THE SOS ONE-PAGE PROPOSAL METHOD

1. The one-page proposal is the ultimate tool for drawing out client objections, which must be addressed in order to close a sale. It serves to immediately focus the conversation on the client's business.

2. A one-sheet helps you organize your thinking. It serves as a script, or notes for you. You are less likely to omit an important point. You appear more professional and are more likely to impress the client. In fact, by following this method, your presentation skills will become greatly enhanced. It helps develop your thinking in a more straightforward and logical way.

3. You are bringing a legitimate idea, something of value, to the meeting. Most media salespeople show up either empty-handed or, often worse, armed with a confusing and generic media kit. Your one-page proposal helps you look like you've done your homework. Here's a rule: The one with the agenda controls the meeting.

4. Each time you work on a one-sheet, you become more of an expert in different customer business categories because you know more about how that particular business works. When you know your client's gross profit margin and average sale, you also know the gross profit margin and average sale for all of his competitors as well. You might also notice that several businesses in that client's product/service category encounter the same frustrations from national competitors.

FIRST, ASK THE RIGHT SEVEN QUESTIONS

Your proposal will contain information that you have gleaned from your client. While I'm educating clients about modern marketing and branding, the difference between good and bad advertising, and how to calculate return on investment, I also ask the client specific questions in order to glean information that I'll need to help my client advertise more efficiently and effectively on my station. Here are the seven questions you must ask your client in order to create a good proposal:

1. What are you doing in the way of advertising and marketing?
2. Why are you doing it?
3. Who are you trying to reach?
4. What do those people you're trying to reach know now about your business?
5. What do you want them to know about your business?
6. What is your average sale?
7. What is your gross profit margin?

Even if I think I already know the answers, I still ask clients these questions. Why? Because I need to hear what the client really thinks, from her lips, about marketing and advertising. By asking questions and listening carefully and not doing all of the talking, I learn a lot about my client's level of ignorance about what I do for a living. When I ask good questions, I discover holes in her perception about marketing, media, and my station. I also discover many of her strengths and weaknesses, and I might learn a lot about the strengths and weaknesses of her competitors. When I ask about average sale and gross profit margin, I'll get information relating to ROI. Then I'll use that information to come up with a concise custom strategy on one piece of paper. I'll also come up with information that will help me create an effective spot.

Here's a conversation with a brake repair service called Don's Brake Repair that exhibits how to glean information. The information in italics indicate what I'm thinking as I listen to the client.

Salesperson: "Regarding marketing and advertising, what are you currently doing?"

Client: "We use the newspaper and the Yellow Pages."

Salesperson: "Why are you using the newspaper?"

Client: "Because it works. We do coupons."

Observation: *ALL media work.*

Salesperson: "Who are you trying to reach?"

Client: "Well, we're trying to reach everybody."

Observation: *We don't have to reach everybody in a campaign, just a percentage of those people who are on for brake repair. I can deal with that later.*

Salesperson: "Those people you're trying to reach, Don, what would you say that those people know about your business right now?"

Observation: *At this point, the client usually begins opening up. I start recognizing some potential problems.*

Client: "We run a good business here. We have a reputation, especially with women, for being honest, for doing good work, and for installing excellent parts. We were the only game in town. But now we have this national competitor. They are advertising prices I can't touch. But they're using cheap parts, and they can't keep good mechanics."

Salesperson: "Mr. Barnhart, what would you *like* for people to know about your business?"

Observation: *At this stage, the real evangelist inside the client starts to come out. I get a lot of ideas for good scripts from this question.*

Client: "Hey, we get a lot of repeat business. And, we've got older, more experienced employees who really believe in doing good work. They treat our customers' brakes like they'd treat their own. Some of our people have been with us for ten years. We have customers who tell us how the work we did really saved their lives."

Observation: *I'm starting to see a great idea for a spot for this client. Real customers telling real stories about how their brakes saved their lives. "When it comes to your family's brakes, you don't want to go to the lowest bidder, now do you?"*

Salesperson: "What's your average sale?"

Client: "Well, when you consider everything, about $300."

Salesperson: "And, I'm guessing that your gross profit margin is similar to the national average for people in the brake repair business. What, 40 percent?"

Client: "Forty-three percent."

See how much information you can get by asking seven simple questions? Now, let's look at how we'll use that information.

Look at the examples of single-page proposals below.

SITUATION

For the first time in twelve years, local business Don's Brake Repair is seeing a decline in revenues. Much of the revenue decline is because a national brake repair chain just opened several large locations. Don's has two locations and a good clientele but can't match his competitor's cut-rate pricing. Don has, on average, older and more experienced mechanics. He also has a reputation he's developed over the years, particularly with women, for being very honest, communicative, and straightforward. And he uses very good parts. His average sale is around $300. The value for one new customer is very important for him, as he gets a lot of repeat business and referrals. His gross profit margin is 43 percent.

OBJECTIVE

- To position and brand Don's Brake Repair as the shop preferred by more women.

- To help the client come up with an identifiable difference that teaches listeners or viewers how they would directly benefit from doing business with Don's. (Perhaps the fact that more than 60 percent of his business comes from females.)

- To attempt to draw at least forty new customers per week (that's 1/256 of 1 percent of our weekly audience), each spending an average of $300 in order to achieve a minimum of breakeven on our advertising campaign.

STRATEGY
Creative

- Use an emotional headline in our commercial that will instill fear or apprehension in the minds of listeners or viewers who will need brake repair this week. Make a strong point that purchasing cheap brake parts from some companies could result in accidents or inconveniences.

- Tell stories of how Don's actual customers avoided collisions by having high-quality parts from Don's and expert installation from employees who understand the importance of "good brakes when you need them most." Use the line, "When it comes to your family's brakes, you don't want to go with the lowest bidder, now do you?"

- Clearly explain how to get to Don's two locations.

Schedule

- Run ten spots per day on Mondays and Tuesdays, March–(whenever), avoiding weekend-oriented commercial clutter.

- Cost: $970 per week for 6 weeks

Here's another example.

SITUATION

Blaine Electric is a family-run electrical contractor specializing in residential rewiring. Its gross profit margin is 42 percent. Blaine is considering cutting back on newspaper and adding broadcast, because broadcast is less saturated with electrical contractor advertising. Blaine's average sale is $3,000 for fixing electrical problems in older homes. Blaine estimates there are hundreds of older homes that risk house fires as a result of faulty old electrical wiring. Blaine wants to do a better job of branding.

OBJECTIVE

- To take advantage of the hole in the broadcast market. Neither Blaine nor any of his competitors are currently using broadcast to sell residential business. We'll brand Blaine into the minds of our viewers/listeners.

- To scare the heck out of people in older homes with old electrical wiring and sell Blaine's identifiable difference, which is expertise in identifying and solving electrical problems in older homes.

- To attempt to draw at least six new customers per week (with a twenty-spot concentrated schedule) who would spend an average of $3,000. Those six customers would represent 0.01 percent of our weekly audience. This would achieve a close to breakeven on the campaign. An additional three average customers per week (0.013 percent of our weekly audience) with the same schedule would achieve in excess of a 30 percent return on advertising investment.

STRATEGY
Creative

- Use statistics from the local fire department to let people know that a great percentage of house fires in our area last year were caused by faulty electrical wiring.

Schedule

- Run ten spots per day on Saturdays and Sundays, March–April of this year.
- Cost: $3,000 per week for fifty-two weeks

IF AT FIRST YOU DON'T SUCCEED . . .

If your idea is really good and that particular client doesn't buy it, do more research, customize it for a new client, and pitch it again.

As you use this method, you will get better and better at writing and presenting ideas. You will become better at handling client objections, closing, and ultimately managing client expectations.

SITUATION, OBJECTIVE, STRATEGY all on one or two sheets of paper. A concise idea based on client research and logical thinking. Clients love it.

Don't expect to sell your one-page idea in that first meeting. Expect that the client will say no to at least some of the points in your proposal. The idea is for the one-sheet to evoke a response in the form of objections. That's what you want. Be prepared to listen so you can appropriately respond. The client may tell you that nothing about your idea is practical. That's fine, as you will ask questions and find out what the client really does need. All you have to do is revise or rewrite the proposal based on what you have learned from the client. You might even be able to do that on the spot and get the client to initial the changes.

W o r k s h e e t: Creating Concise and Customized Marketing and Advertising Proposals

1. Briefly describe the way you currently write local direct client proposals.

2. Based on this chapter and information you have about a local client, write an SOS proposal now.

CHAPTER

■■■ 20 ■■■

Break Through the Commercial Clutter: Power Presentations

W ho's driving the bus during your client meetings? Is it usually you, or is it more often the client? When you're making a presentation, the onus of communication is entirely upon you. It is your responsibility to make sure that your ideas are communicated in language that solves your client's problems in language that he fully understands. If you want to make big local direct sales, you have to be in charge. You must take the initiative to present in an interesting and logical way, or you'll never break through the 5,000 other commercial impressions per day that your client is being exposed to. You need to lead the way, modifying your client's behavior by educating him in language that he can understand, so that you can both arrive at a mutually beneficial conclusion, which is a long-term schedule on your station. Your chances of closing big sales are greatly diminished if you have poor presentation skills.

I have seen a number of great advertising ideas get flushed because of the seller's utter lack of presentation skills. In a recent case, a presentation was so disorganized that the frustrated client actually threw the account executive out of the room. If you're having problems closing, you'd better take a good look at how you're presenting yourself and your ideas.

Here are some ideas that can help improve your presentation skills.

> *Negotiate when and where.* If you can, try to negotiate the time and the place for your presentation. Try to schedule a time that you're usually at your sharpest and most alert. Negotiate the meeting place, away from your client's business if you can. Try to meet at your station or in a neutral spot where your client won't be distracted by phone calls or other interruptions. Try to choose a place where you can think and listen and feel comfortable. Your station might be the best place. Remember that most people, including local direct clients, have never been to a broadcast facility before. So invite your clients to the station where you can control the environment. You can feel like a big shot, introducing your client to air staff and management.

> *If winging it is your plan, prepare for unpleasant surprises during your meeting.* With no firm agenda for the meeting, the client might take the opportunity to vent and drop a few bombs on you and your station. Remember, the person with the agenda controls the meeting. For that reason I suggest you use your SOS proposal as your notes. It will serve as your presentation guide so that you can stay focused. It should help you tell a good, well-organized story, with a beginning, a middle, and an end, about how your plan is absolutely in the client's best interest and point out the ways your ideas identify and solve specific client problems.

> *Take command when it's your turn to speak.* Exude enthusiasm. Your excitement helps create desire for your idea. Try to stand while making your pitch. Smile, speak clearly, and use gestures to help make your points. Go over your proposal point by point; be prepared to stop at any time and answer objections. When you have answered the objection, go back to the proposal and continue following your agenda to a logical and mutually beneficial conclusion.

It should go without saying that any time you meet with clients or potential clients you want to look and act like the sharpest tool in the shed. Nose rings and other facial piercings may be cool at night and on weekends, but take them out before your client appointment. Reason: Why would you give anybody any reason not to buy? You want your client focusing on what you have to say, not on your pierced tongue. Dressing up is almost always better than dressing down.

The best presenters feel comfortable in virtually any situation. They don't mind hearing client objections. They don't freak out if a computer or a projector or some other piece of equipment fails because they know the material so well they don't need props. The best presenters expect the unexpected. I've had fire alarms go off during a presentation. I've had all kinds of interruptions. And of course, I've had the occasional "curveball" question. With practice and confidence you will get to the point that you can feel comfortable enough in any situation so that you can roll with anything that might occur and still manage to get back on track.

Many years ago I decided I could use some help with presentations. I talked with several heavy-hitting closers and found that three of them had something in common. Toastmasters. That's right, Toastmasters clubs. Virtually every community in the civilized world has a local chapter. Toastmasters' only goal is to help you become a better speaker, in both one-on-one conversations and in front of groups. I can't begin to tell you how much you'll learn from a Toastmasters' group about the power of persuasion, extemporaneous thinking skills, how to organize your thinking, and how to improve your basic communication skills. It's inexpensive, it's fun, and you'll learn so many things that will help you make money.

You have two ears and one mouth for a reason. Be a good listener at all times. If you see or hear something that you don't fully understand, ask the person you are pitching to please repeat or restate what they have said. Again, always listen carefully.

Probe for information when you don't understand a prospect's point. "When you say that, you mean . . . ?" and let the client finish the statement or thought so that you understand precisely what your client is trying to say. Be prepared to listen hard. Sometimes in conversation we're so wrapped up in what we want to say that we don't really hear what the other person is saying, or trying to say.

Record your presentation so you can see what your client sees. Get someone to videotape your pitch before you actually deliver it to a client. Watch for any obvious distractions. Do you say, "Um," or "Ah," or "you know" too much? Look for continuity. Are you telling a good story? Are you following the agenda? Is it exciting? If not, then perhaps you should add more enthusiasm.

Are you identifying and solving real problems for your client? You have all of the tools you need to put together a compelling story about marketing, branding, the difference between good and bad advertising, and why long-term advertising with you is a good, calculated risk instead of a gamble.

You and only you are your idea's biggest advocate. Your presentation must convey your enthusiasm to your client. Then you will answer her questions and close your sale. You will learn more about handling objections and closing in upcoming chapters.

W o r k s h e e t: Break Through the Commercial Clutter: Power Presentations

The purpose of this worksheet is to help you to develop a more effective client presentation.

1. Based on what you've learned in this chapter, write down a definite course of action (i.e., research, scheduling, proposal preparation) you'll begin taking immediately to improve the quality of your presentations.

CHAPTER
■■■ **21** ■■■

How to Negotiate Without Turning into a Pitiful Puddle of Spineless Goo

Let us never negotiate out of fear. And, let us never fear to negotiate.   John F. Kennedy

In the Czech Republic some people still remember old communist jokes. In one such joke two brothers are split up in 1968 after one flees to Germany and the other remains in Czechoslovakia. The brother in Germany prospers while his sibling endures the hardships of communist oppression. Years later they secretly meet in the forest. The brother living in Germany asks his brother, "So, how is it going with the Russians?" His brother replies, "Oh, quite well. You see, we made a 'deal' with the Russians. They take all of our manufactured goods." His brother asks, "Well, what do you get in exchange?" The sibling answers, "In exchange, we give them all of our natural resources and free labor."

In this case, any "negotiating" on the Czech's part was done under extreme duress. Thankfully, it's a rare day when broadcast sellers have to negotiate a buy with armed clients.

Some of us in broadcasting think we're better at negotiating than a lot of other industries. Oh, yeah? Then where did posting come from? Wouldn't you have liked to have been a fly on the wall at the very first posting meeting between an agency person and a tv general manager?

Agency: "We're going to change the way we buy television. From now on, we're going to buy your station based on the ratings you have now. But if your ratings drop, then you owe us."

TV Manager: "Okay. I think I understand. So if our ratings go up, then you owe us?"

Agency: "No."

TV Manager: "Okay, I do understand. We'll do it!"

Brilliant. Hey, radio people, don't laugh too loud. How many free appearances and bonus spots have you given away lately? And be careful, major agencies are still trying to get radio stations to start posting as well.

SUCCESSFUL NEGOTIATING IS NOT DIFFICULT

Negotiation is merely a learned skill that, if practiced regularly, becomes a natural instinct. Negotiation is simply the art of modifying the behavior of another person toward a mutually beneficial conclusion. So, why does it have to be so awkward? Why do we feel we have to give up so soon?

Most media salespeople are the worst negotiators in the world. As soon as a buyer puts on any pressure, the salesperson falls apart. Instead of negotiating with the client, we end up negotiating with our sales manager. In some countries, you have to pay bribes to advertising agencies to get their business. Here in the United States we call this "added value." We routinely give away added value and bonus spots. In fact, agency buys seldom come down without stipulating value-added guarantees.

Shamefully, this disturbing trend is now raising its ugly head with direct clients and it's no wonder. Anxious to add billing, salespeople in every market size are actually volunteering added value, without the client even asking. Do you enjoy working for free? Wouldn't you rather drink paint than spend one more Saturday hanging around at free remotes?

ANYBODY CAN GIVE IT AWAY

As in other industries, the broadcast salesperson will always take the path of what he or she believes offers the least resistance in closing a deal. Anybody can give it away; however, it takes a real salesperson to sell it. You don't have to cave during a negotiation. You work hard in this business and there is no logical reason why you shouldn't be paid well for your hard work.

Some tips for much better negotiation:

1. **Don't haggle over price.** Rate resistance comes from a lack of perception of value. Try to keep the discussion focused on your value and benefit to your client, not your price. There is no question that value can be perceived completely differently between two individuals, depending on the education of both sides. It is always in your best interest to make sure that you understand as much as possible about how your client's business works. Of course, it's equally important that you educate your client on the benefits of marketing and advertising and how valuable your audience is to your client's bottom line. Steer your client away from price and back toward value. For example, what's the value of one new customer to your client?

2. **Start high.** Propose bigger schedules. How much is the client spending in the Yellow Pages or in the newspaper? Remind the client that with you she could own a day or a daypart or a program. That's virtually impossible to do in the newspaper, even with a full-page ad.

3. **Ask for a long-term contract.** If you don't ask for long-term business, you won't get a long-term contract. Asking for a long-term contract is so easy. Instead of proposing a local direct schedule for just a week or a month, suggest a schedule that runs every week of the year. Why wouldn't you? What's the worst thing that could happen to you if you asked a client for a long-term commitment? I did some

research, and last year, not one single broadcast salesperson was tortured and killed for asking a client to sign a long-term contract.

It's this simple. After you've finished with your presentation and you've answered all objections, you could say something like this:

> "Okay, Mr. Client. We've agreed that owning Tuesdays and Saturdays on our station is logical. We'll fish this lake for customers who are on right now for what you're selling and we'll start the process of branding others. So, let's own Tuesdays and Saturdays. The weekly cost is _____. We might alter the schedule during holiday weeks, but otherwise we own these days. Just sign here and I'll get this schedule locked in for you."

If the client says no this time, find out what the objection is, educate the client, and ask the next time. If the client says no again, find out why, educate the client correctly, and ask again. You have nothing to lose by always asking for an annual contract.

As they say, "It is better to be rich and healthy than poor and sick." Having long-term contracts means that you start each month with a substantial base of business rather than having to start over from zero every month. Long-term contracts are the way to get rich in this business. But if you want long-term commitments, you have to ask for them.

Use a long-term contract as leverage in your negotiation. In other words, consider conceding on a minor point in exchange for a longer-term order.

4. **Have confidence.** Before you sit down with your client, visualize a successful negotiation. Have confidence in your ability to come out of the meeting with a few victories and a good, solid deal. You represent thousands and thousands of pairs of eyes and ears with legs and wallets. Your audience has tremendous value to your client, and *you* have

value to your client. Your knowledge of marketing and advertising means you know how to successfully modify the behavior of a percentage of those thousands of consumers your station represents. So, have confidence in your ability to negotiate a good deal for you and your client. You're not just a Pitiful Puddle of Spineless Goo. You could be a valuable asset to your client. You're good enough, you're smart enough, and by gosh, people like you.

5. **Everybody wins.** A successful negotiation is not a game with a winner and a loser. In order to have a successful negotiation, both sides must feel as though they have won. You are not there to destroy an opponent. Nor are you there to be destroyed. You are there to strike a deal where everybody believes that he or she has won something. Remember that you are working toward a common goal.

6. **Don't waste time with the wrong person.** Have you ever spent valuable time and/or money dealing with someone who was not the decision maker? It gets you so mad you just want to stab yourself in the neck. To make absolutely sure you're dealing with the person who buys the advertising, *ASK*. Ask the person directly if he or she is the person who buys the advertising for the company. If the real decision maker can't be there, try to reschedule until you can meet with the correct person. In fact, be sure to ask the non-decision maker to help you arrange an appointment with the real decision maker.

7. **Never judge a book by its cover.** . . . Or a client by his or her appearance or manner. Always assume that your client is as skilled a negotiator as you are. Don't underestimate anybody and you'll have fewer surprises.

8. **What's your client's motivation?** Do some homework before your meeting and try your best to figure out what your client's primary motivation will be in the negotiation. It may not be what you think it is. It may or may not be rate. It may or may not be added value. It may or may not be a

better creative idea. It may or may not be a trip or other incentive.

9. **Teach your client that you're the good guy.** Have short- and long-term goals of building a foundation of trust and confidence with your client. Don't lie or cheat or cover something up. If you make a mistake, admit it, apologize, make amends, and move on. Always behave in a way that is absolutely beyond reproach. Work toward establishing a relationship where what you say goes unquestioned. This doesn't necessarily mean that your client will agree with everything you say, only that he or she would perceive you as honest.

10. **Gray is okay.** Remember that in a good negotiation, nothing is black and white. There should always be some gray space. Deals are made in the gray spaces.

11. **Don't get emotional.** Try to look at every possible side of a deal, every angle and detail, before and during the negotiation. Your ability to stay objective and flexible will be crucial to the outcome. If you are emotionally attached to any single issue, your ability to negotiate objectively is compromised. Don't fight to win a battle then lose the war. That's being pig-headed. Sacrifice smaller points to win bigger ones.

12. **Keep it simple.** Try to guide the meeting agenda and stick to a simple plan. Keep your agenda as simple and straightforward as possible. Use the SOS one-sheet proposal as your agenda. Remember KISS? *Keep It Simple Stupid.* The more complicated the proposal, the tougher the close.

13. **Turn your weaknesses into strengths.** For example, if you look young, don't let your youth be mistaken for lack of experience or ability. The same goes with your race, your gender, your handicap, or any other issue that you think may be perceived as a weakness. Subtly point out your strengths and skills early in the discussion. If you're young, for example, older clients might appreciate your youthful perspective when it comes to marketing their products or services to a younger audience.

14. **The offense scores the points.** If you're dealing with a notoriously tough negotiator, and you've never been good with bullies, try to go on the offensive first. If the client owes you money or didn't quite do what he said he would do the last time you had an agreement, bring those things up early and throw him off his rhythm.

15. **Don't sweat the petty stuff.** Always know exactly what you can or can't offer. If your client asks for small concessions and isn't moving on the bigger issue until you agree to his, and you know that you have the flexibility to add the concession, quickly say, "Let's add that."

16. **Look 'em in the eye.** Maintain good eye contact. Practice. Try looking at only one of the client's eyes if that makes you feel more comfortable (the client will not be able to tell from across the table). If you don't believe me, try it for yourself. Sit across a table from a person and stare at just one eye. Ask the other person if he or she can tell.

17. **Don't attack a grizzly bear.** Professional negotiators learn early on that when principle is involved, don't attack the principle. For example, don't try to tell a fundamental newspaper client that the newspaper doesn't work. That's just plain stupid. Instead, educate your client on the value of using a media mix. By adding a schedule on your station, your client will reach more potential customers that do not read the paper. And mentioning the newspaper ad in your commercial (BE SURE TO LOOK AT OUR AD IN THE SPORTS SECTION OF TODAY'S PAPER) will cause more readers to notice the client's print ad.

18. **Kiss and make up.** Never allow a misunderstanding or a personality issue to get tangled up in a business negotiation. If you and your client have underlying issues or dramas, talk about them and clear them up. Bring the facts out in the open. If the client deserves an apology, apologize and move on.

19. **Three's a crowd.** If the client brings a third party into the negotiation, or you have to get a decision by committee, it usually spells disaster. Seldom has anyone ever gotten every single storeowner in a shopping center to agree to do an advertising campaign.

20. **Negotiate everything.** Ask, ask, ask. Most clients will concede and pay for a number of things that they assume are free, or that you would normally give away for free.

   - Negotiate a fee for promotional mentions.
   - Negotiate for more money per paid spot to help pay the cost of the promotion.
   - Negotiate to split the cost for tee shirts, calendars, and other promotional items.
   - Negotiate with the client to get your station featured in all of the client's other advertising.
   - Negotiate with the client to pay for newspaper ads or direct mail you'll have to do, including printing, point of purchase, catering, and any other promotional costs.
   - Negotiate with the client to provide substantial prizes, things that listeners or viewers will really want to win.
   - Negotiate with the client to hang your banners in highly visible locations inside and outside the store and to play your station for at least a week ahead of the promotion.
   - Ask the client to help provide you with other vendors to help with the cost of the promotion.
   - Negotiate a fee for engineers and setup.
   - Negotiate talent fees for live appearances.
   - Insist on a longer-term contract before agreeing to any added value.

21. **Put it in writing.** To avoid misunderstandings, always follow up an oral negotiation with a written agreement.

The bottom line is that most clients will respect you more when you negotiate like a professional. Don't make everything so easy to get. Help your client perceive that your station has value. Negotiate for everything. Everything should have a price. Don't allow the client to think for a minute that anything is free. Everything you have has value and can be used to negotiate a better situation for you and your company.

W o r k s h e e t: How to Negotiate Without Turning into a Pitiful Puddle of Spineless Goo

The purpose of this worksheet is to help us become better negotiators.

1. Think about a current local direct client you'd like to upgrade to a long-term contract. Based on your previous dealings with that client, what kinds of demands do you think he or she would make before signing your agreement? How would you respond to those demands?

2. Describe how you could immediately incorporate some of the things you learned in this chapter to improve your negotiating skills.

CHAPTER

■■■ 22 ■■■

Why Objections Are Our Friends and Logical Ways to Handle Them

Many broadcast salespeople become intimidated by clients because we don't feel comfortable with client objections. This is absolutely unforgivable, especially for broadcast sales veterans. As we'll learn, most objections to broadcast advertising are the same. We'll look at those objections and how to answer them intelligently. Practice answering objections so that when you hear one, you know precisely what to say. And always remember that objections are good, not bad. We cannot close a sale if a client still has objections; however, we can usually address the objections to the client's satisfaction. Most client objections come from ignorance. Our job is to ferret out the objection and educate the client correctly. For us, the objective is the objection.

As a brand new salesperson I was intimidated by objections. I still believed that no meant NO. A NO from a client was as negative as the old NO from my parents. Consequently, I took nos very personally— until I got smarter. Gradually, I came to understand that objections are a good thing. If you don't have objections and answer them satisfactorily, then you won't close the sale. I learned that when it comes to sales, objections are usually born from ignorance. That means that when it comes to the selling process, no doesn't necessarily mean no. Most of the time it simply means that I've got a little more work to do.

If we do our jobs correctly, we might just see our clients go from "NO" to "No" to "no" to "maybe" to "possibly" to "YES."

Don't be intimidated by clients. They are just humans, made up of skin, hair, guts, bones, and blood just like us. We can help them solve major problems. Instead of being intimidated, we must listen carefully and answer objections clearly and confidently.

Most local direct clients already have the perception that what we do for a living is complicated, confusing, and expensive. If the client thinks that broadcast advertising is just a crapshoot, he sees no value in doing business with us. Clearly, we do have value to clients. We represent thousands of potential customers for our clients. Our job is to fish out client objections so we can properly educate the client and close the sale. Educated clients buy more than uneducated clients and that's a fact.

MOST OBJECTIONS ARE RELATIVELY THE SAME

Most objections to media salespeople are relatively the same and, on occasion, you'll get something from way out in left field. The one element that the most familiar objections have in common is that, for the most part, they arise from ignorance. The client raises objections because you have not yet properly educated her about advertising and marketing, the difference between good and bad advertising, and how to calculate ROI. The onus is by and large on the salesperson, not the client.

Keep in mind that in a perfect world a successful business would have a marketing triangle that looks like an equilateral triangle or a pyramid. All three sides would be equal. On the left side you'd have product or service, on the right side you'd have sales force, and across the bottom you'd have advertising. However, most marketing triangles usually wind up looking more like a witch's hat than an equilateral triangle. The side that says advertising is usually the weakest link. Why? It's the most mysterious side. It's the hardest side to quantify. It's the hardest side to qualify. It's the side that most business people know the least about and that's our fault.

Here are some common broadcast objections and some good ways to handle them.

1. **"Word of mouth is the best kind of advertising."**
   "I couldn't agree with you more. Word of mouth is an excellent form of advertising. Radio and television advertising is controlled word of mouth. You control the words. This is important to understand, Ms. Client, because there is good word of mouth and sometimes there is bad word of mouth. For example, if you go to a restaurant and get an okay meal, you might tell a couple of people. But if you go to a restaurant and get a bad meal, who are you going to tell, then? *Everybody.* All businesses make mistakes. One employee could destroy a fifty year reputation. One of the reasons you must maintain a consistent advertising schedule is to help put out those little fires of insurrection that develop when somebody had a bad experience with your business. Controlled word of mouth is like a layer of insulation for your business. It's like insurance to help fight bad word of mouth."

2. **"I tried it once and it didn't work."**
   "Well, if you really believe that it doesn't work, then I guess you won't mind if I spend my own money and buy a campaign on our station next week advertising that you're going out of business, and everything in your store is now 85 percent off!" But, that's the snippy way to answer the question. Look, you need to teach your clients that all media are good. Newspaper is good. Billboards are good. Radio and television are good. The Yellow Pages are good. However, media must be used correctly in order to work for the client.

   "I tried it once and it didn't work," is a sign that one or several things were wrong with his campaign. It is your job to determine why the client believes this and then educate him that all media are good. Did the client run on the wrong station or the wrong program for his demographic? Did the client run a weak schedule? Look at the creative. Was it written by a crapmaster? No headline; filled with clichés that nobody hears; call to action, phone number, or address mentioned only once and then obscured with a cliché slogan at the end? Does the client have marketing problems? Is it really hard to get his product or service, even if you try? Is his phone always busy? Is the product or service something ridiculous that nobody would really want? Is it overpriced? Poorly packaged? Or were his expectations about results mismanaged from the beginning? Is it possible that the client had more than one of these problems at the same time? I've actually met clients who had all of these problems at the same time. No wonder they think that radio or television advertising don't work.

You'll have to figure out the problem, educate the client properly, and, with your good logic, advice, and a little patience, maybe you'll be able to get the client back on the air with a solid and reasonable campaign.

3. **"We've got more business than we can handle."**

   "That's great. When are you expanding?" is one thing you could say. More often though, you're beating your head against the wall. Sometimes clients really do have more business than they can handle. That means it's time to go to that client's direct competitor and say, "So-and-so has more business than he can handle and you don't. Because your competitor is cutting back, now would be a great time to start branding and capturing mind share among our listeners/viewers. You'll have less competition on our station right now. I wonder how many of your competitor's excess clientele we could convert to your business this year."

4. **"You're not number one."**

   Here's another common objection from clients who have been trained to believe your station has no value unless you're number one. Clearly this is another misconception born of ignorance, and here's a great way to deflect that misconception. "You know, you're not number one in your industry, either. And I don't have to be number one in mine. I still represent thousands of consumers who will buy your product/service from somebody this week. How difficult are you making it for them to buy from you, when you don't teach them who you are, what you do, and how to get in touch with you?"

5. **"I've seen your ratings and you don't have any listeners/viewers."**

Ah . . . so, your competitor has taken it upon himself to educate your client about radio or television ratings information and slam your station in the process. This is a no-no with direct clients. You should never bad-mouth another radio station or another medium. You'll need to draw out the objection. Obviously, your station has an audience. Listen carefully to the client and find out exactly what the client has heard. Then, in a calm way, explain that, unfortunately, the salesperson at the other station is misinformed. Build a case for the audience that you do have. Point out the strengths that your audience has, that it matches the client's demographic, and then get back to building value for your idea. Offer to provide the client with the names and phone numbers of other clients that you have had success with. This will usually get the ball rolling. Then, try to answer the objection the same way you would for "You're not number one."

6. **"I only use the newspaper (or Yellow Pages)."**

The newspaper is a great medium. And always remember that all media are good. You'll seldom get anywhere trying to sell an avid newspaper or Yellow Pages client on dropping that medium to give yours a shot. Obviously, the client believes that the newspaper works and may be ignorant about the benefits your medium, which works just as well, could bring to his or her business. Here are some things you could say to begin the education process. "You use the newspaper (or Yellow Pages)? That's great, because I'm in the newspaper (or Yellow Pages) advertising business as well. Mixing media is a logical idea, and I'll advertise your newspaper (or Yellow Pages) ad on our radio/television station. You'll get even better results by reminding our thousands of consumers to be sure and take a good look at your newspaper (or Yellow Pages) ad. Your ad will stand out more when we tell our listeners or viewers where to find your ad and what it looks like."

When a client tells you he only uses the newspaper or the Yellow Pages, remind him that a significant number of his competitors are also using the newspaper (or Yellow Pages). "Mr. Client, the newspaper (or Yellow Pages) is a great advertising medium. It's a big lake with a lot of fish. But with your particular product or service category, wouldn't you agree that the newspaper (or Yellow Pages) is a little oversaturated? It looks to me like every one of your competitors is fishing on the same lake. My lake also has thousands of fish in it, and we don't have one single advertiser from your product or service category fishing on our lake. Heck, right now, you'd have practically a monopoly fishing on our lake."

You could point out that in the newspaper's own studies it was revealed that decreasing the size of an ad does not mean a proportionate decrease in people viewing that same ad. In other words, going from a full-page ad to a three-quarter-page ad is a more efficient way to use newspaper. And with a three-quarter-page ad, the page is actually more interesting because the paper will run a story in the remaining space. "The dollars you shave off that big ad would go a long way on our station in helping you promote your event and the location of your newspaper ad."

There is a huge hole you should point out to your clients who buy big ads in the Yellow Pages. The problem is that most people flip through the Yellow Pages from back to front. That means that when they get to your client's category, they get to shop the smaller ads first.

7. **"I'm just not ready to do anything right now."**

"Let me think about it" is not a concluded negotiation. This vague statement could mean several things. One thing it definitely means is that your client is harboring hidden objections about your proposal. It could mean that the client is just trying to blow you off and doesn't know what else to say. Instead of just taking the statement at face value and saying, "Okay, but be sure and call me when you're ready" (the client will never call you), try to find out what the real objection really is.

One thing I've discovered many, many times is that when the client says he's not ready to do anything right now, he means *right now*. That is to say, it's not logical to assume that just because you popped in for a visit in the middle of a month that the client has the budget to advertise with you right now. I've gotten buys by simply asking when the client would be ready. Hey, maybe she means she'll have the budget two months from now. That's fine. Take the advance order now.

Or to bring out the client's real objection quickly, just say, "Ms. Client, we have thousands of potential customers out there who will buy what you're selling from somebody this week. Is there another reason why you wouldn't want to start educating them about who you are, what you do, and how to get in touch with you immediately, so that they would have the option to do business with you, instead of with your competitors?"

8. **"I don't like your format/programming/music."**

This objection can be easily handled using this logic. "I'm glad you brought that up, and I appreciate how you feel. But have you ever been fishing? Well, if you wanted to catch fish, would you bait your hook with food you like to eat, or food that the fish like? I might not like everything on our station either, but thousands and thousands of other consumers obviously do. How difficult are you making it for them to buy from you when they don't know who you are, what you do, or how to get in touch with you? Let's go fishing!"

9. **"Your rates are too high."**

This is a classic objection in any line of sales work. Find out exactly what the client means by "too high" in order to put things into perspective. Obviously, he doesn't fully comprehend the value of your expertise in bringing customers to his business. The price is always the first objection when the client doesn't understand the value you bring to his business. Did you show the client how to calculate return on investment? Based on his average sale and his gross profit margin, how many new customers must your campaign bring in for the client to break even on what he's spending with you? And, what is the value of one new customer to our client? A grocery store for example, operates on a 20 percent gross profit margin. Say its average sale is close to $100. How long have you been going to the same grocer? One year? Two years? Longer? How often do you visit your grocer? Twice, or three times per week? If someone moved into your neighborhood and asked you to recommend a grocery store, would you recommend yours? The value of one new customer to your grocer could be thousands of dollars over a few short years. How big is your total weekly audience? Doesn't it seem logical that with a good spot and a logical schedule, that a percentage of your audience might be looking for a new grocer this week?

The value of one new customer to your client could be very significant. Your rate, in comparison, might look very insignificant based on what your station could ultimately do for that client.

10. **"The budget is already allocated."**

    You know, sometimes you just show up at the wrong time of the year. It might be possible to convince your client to "steal" some budget for you from another area, like sales or PR. Or, you might be able to scare up some "free money" in the way of co-op money. Or, you might be able to steal some of the client's other media budget. However, it is likely that you might have a problem getting this client on the air this time. Many clients plan their advertising budgets in October or November for the following year. If you missed this year's opportunity to pitch for this business, make sure you get an appointment early, in time to work for next year's budget.

11. **Don't waste too much time with contentious clients.**

    Remember what we said earlier? "The best thing about beating your head against the wall is that it feels so good when you stop." That means don't spend too much time with argumentative or rate-spoiled clients. There are too many other local direct clients in your signal coverage area, hundreds or thousands of them, who need to be educated about the value of advertising with your station. Rate-spoiled clients may never buy from you, even though you've answered every objection. If you sense that a relationship is going nowhere, fire the contentious client and move on!

W o r k s h e e t: Why Objections Are Our Friends and Logical Ways to Handle Them

- Objections are a good thing—objections and opinions show an interest in the proposal.
- Become comfortable with handling objections and answering them with confidence.

Number from 1 to 10 (1 being most often heard) the following most common and familiar objections that you've experienced while involved in media sales. Discuss how to counter these objections.

a. _____ I tried it once and it didn't work.

b. _____ Word of mouth is the best kind of advertising for us.

c. _____ You're not number one.

d. _____ I've seen your ratings and you don't have any listeners/viewers.

e. _____ I only use the newspaper.

f. _____ I already have more business than I can handle.

g. _____ I'm just not ready to do anything right now.

h. _____ I don't like your format/programming/music.

i. _____ Your rates are too high.

j. _____ The budget is already allocated.

CHAPTER
■■■ 23 ■■■

How to Close Broadcast Sales Without Looking Like a Jerk

Failure to close a sale is like cooking an excellent meal and then never bothering to taste it. It's like climbing a mountain to watch a glorious sunset, then looking east instead of west. What's the point of doing all of the work and then not reaping the reward? Selling is the modification of the behavior of another person. It is your job to guide the prospect to a mutually beneficial conclusion. The onus to close is entirely on you. Rarely does the client close himself. If you don't ask for the order, you won't get the order. And as long as you're asking for something, why not ask for a long-term contract?

This chapter is all about closing. We'll give you several techniques for drawing out objections and closing the sale. Objections to broadcast advertising are a good thing. That means that your prospect is interested enough in your proposal to have questions. Or, he or she has an opinion about it. Perhaps this opinion is based on ignorance about advertising or marketing or your station. It's your job to flush these things out so that you can educate your client properly. Remember that educated clients buy more than uneducated clients.

The importance of learning how to always ask for long-term local direct business is essential to the survival of our stations.

Reason: By not asking local direct clients for long-term business, we are setting ourselves up to fail in many ways.

- Wasted time and effort.
- Higher broadcast sales turnover.
- No client loyalty.
- Starting every month with zero on the books.
- Losing business to thieves from little agencies and other stations.
- No real chance at building long-term client trust.
- Repeated problems with rate resistance.
- Surprise cancellations.
- Availability problems—you can never get good schedules.
- We look like pests instead of resources.

Let's explore the logic of why we should, in every single case, ask for a long-term commitment and why, if we don't get that commitment this time, we should ask the next time and the next time and the next time.

WHAT'S IN IT FOR YOU?

- *Security on many levels.* You cannot get rich in this business unless you have long-term business. If you don't have long contracts, you start every month with a big, fat zero. You are out on the streets in the middle of a broadcast month, beating your head against a wall trying to get clients to sign up for a week or two with money they haven't budgeted. With several long-term customers you've got money in the bank. You start a month with thousands on the books. Anything you add after the month has started is gravy. Your boss loves you, and you're making lots of money. Salespeople who make lots of money are unlikely to quit or get fired. What will you do with all of that money? Retire rich someday? Or would you rather wind up living under a bridge somewhere snacking in dumpsters for sustenance? If you prefer being rich, then ask for the long-term business every single time. It makes sense.

- *You keep the vultures away from your clients.* Without a signed, long-term agreement, you have no insurance against theft. Your friends at the little agencies and from other media will see or hear your client on your station and go after your account. Without the long-term agreement, you are vulnerable, and the vultures will eventually pick you clean. With the long-term contract, your client is locked in with you, immunizing you against parasites from little agencies and the other stations. With a long-term contract your budget is entered into the client's computer. Paying your station is as automatic as paying the light bill or the phone bill.

- *You become a resource to the client, instead of a pest.* Imagine that I worked for a sales company that sold soap and that every time you saw me I was trying to sell you soap or trying to recruit you into my sales organization. What would you do if you saw me coming? "Run, Forrest, RUN!" And, what if you had a "gatekeeper" or secretary, and he told you that I was holding on the phone for you? He or she would say, "It's that soap guy Paul Weyland again. Do you want to talk to him?" What would you say? You would LIE to keep from talking to me. Without the long-term contract, every time the client sees you coming, you have your hand out asking for money. You're just like the little chiquita girls in Mexico. "Por favor, are you doing anything this month? You ran with us last month. Por favor, just a little something?" Every time you see your client, you bring with you the implied threat of asking for money. You're no fun to see any more.

- *You could build a life-long client relationship.* With a long-term agreement, your visit turns into a treat. Every time the clients see you, you have valuable information on competitors, or you're there to help them when they're short-handed. Or possibly, you're providing them with concert tickets, CDs, DVDs, and other perks from the entertainment industry. In a way, you become the client's conduit to the fabulous world of the entertainment industry. And, with the monthly chiquita imitation out of the way, you can begin building a working friendship that lasts years, even a lifetime. You enter the client's "circle of trust," one of those professional people who stay in the client's life for the long term, like his doctor, dentist, lawyer, insurance agent, tax consultant, or stockbroker. You transcend the business relationship level and move on to the status of trusted professional friend. If a chiquita from another station tried to take your business away or said anything derogatory about you or your station, your client would come to your defense.

CLOSING DOESN'T HAVE TO BE SLEAZY

Closing is simply using subtle ways to look for buying signals (interest in your proposal) and then draw out any objections.

Look at good retail salespeople and the natural way they guide your behavior. "Can I take that to the counter for you?" "Why don't you try that on?" "Can I wrap that up for you?" "Would you like to wear that out?" All of these questions are designed to help draw out objections and close retail customers. In broadcast sales, we too have tools for ferreting out objections and closing deals.

NATURAL CLOSING TECHNIQUES

Here are some of my favorite closing techniques. They are all logical and natural ways to flush out any remaining objections and guide your client toward your common goal. Customize the close for your personality style and the personality of the person you are dealing with. Make closing easy and natural for both you and the client. Each selling situation might be different. As we'll see, mixing several closing techniques is usually best.

- **Direct close:** Just ask for the business. "Let's do it." Nike uses the slogan, "Just Do It." After finishing your presentation you would simply say, "Hey, let's do it," and then wait for any objections.

- **Summary close:** Once you've finished your presentation and you realize you haven't gotten any client objections, go through your proposal again point by point. If you get an objection, stop and deal with it, then continue your summary until you have finished. Then say, "Let's do it."

- **Assumptive close:** From the beginning of the presentation, you assume that the client is going to buy. You start with, "Here's what we're going to do." If there is an objection—for example if your client says, "Whoa, wait just a minute. We're not doing anything yet"—apologize for being overeager, identify the objection, handle it, and then use the summary or direct close.

- **SRO close:** Standing Room Only creates a sense of urgency. "I recommend that if we want to own Mondays and Tuesdays, let's lock this schedule in now so that we don't run into inventory problems down the road." You'll notice that I used the words, "Let's lock this schedule in now." This expression helps convey a sense of urgency to the client. If you publish avails (a report showing what times are still available and those that are already sold), it is helpful to bring them with you when you visit the client so that he can see for himself that your inventory is getting tight.

- **Minor point close:** Close the client on minor elements of the proposal. "Do you want to start on Tuesday or Saturday?" Or, "I like both spots, but I like the way spot #2 begins. Which one sounds most logical to you?"

- **Make me an offer close:** This is a last resort close designed for the client who says your proposal is too expensive. It helps keep the client from saying no and allows you a continuing dialog, so that you can defend your proposal. "Well, if this is too expensive, what do you think it's worth?" Obviously, you won't sell the schedule for what the client thinks it's worth, but this technique helps you establish that at least the client perceives some value in your proposition. Clearly in the client's mind you have not finished conveying the value of your audience over price. Go over ROI again until the client perceives value over price.

- **The pen close:** This close is used frequently by people in the automotive and the insurance businesses. It's an intriguing psychological exercise, and I've seen it work many times. Once you've made your presentation, you say, "Let's do it." You then place the contract and a pen in front of the client. If the client has no objections, he or she typically says something like, "Well, I guess this is where I sign," and then signs your agreement. Other times, the client will pick up the pen and start twirling and playing with it. This action indicates that the client is still in the game but has some questions or objections. As you systematically handle remaining questions or objections, the client will sign the contract. If you don't ferret out and handle all remaining objections, then the client won't sign the contract.

Use multiple closes. For example, you might start with the assumptive close, telling the client immediately, "Look, here's what we're going to do." If you don't hear an objection after you've gone over your proposal, use the direct close and say, "Let's do it." If the client just sits and says nothing, use the summary close. Go back over your SOS proposal and say, "Well, I think we agree on the situation. Now here's the objective, strategy (etc.)," and try to determine the objection. Remember to ask for the long-term business. It is absolutely in your best interest to do so. Launch into it at the beginning of your presentation with an assumptive close like this: "Ms. Client, I'm here to help you set up a five-year marketing and advertising program. We will break that down into annual increments so we can evaluate progress." It's amazing how many clients will begin to nod their heads in agreement with this long-term approach. They're looking for someone who knows what he or she is doing to drive the bus.

Close early and close often during your presentation. It's not difficult and it's not cheesy. It's natural, and it must be done. You must educate your client, ferret out objections, and then ask for the order. If you don't, all of your hard work was for nothing. Use several closing techniques, draw out all objections and go from **NO** to No to no to maybe to **YES!**

Practice and use these closes. If you don't, you're like a ship without a rudder. You're just treading water. You "ain't goin' nowhere." And if you don't know where you're going, any road will get you there. Salespeople who don't know how to close eventually quit out of frustration or get fired.

HUGE SUGGESTION

When the client says yes, you must leave as quickly as possible. If you stay, the client may get buyer's remorse and change his or her mind or revise the amount he or she agreed to spend with you. After the client signs the contract, get up and leave. Your business is done for the time being and the client has other things to do. Say, "Thank you very much. I'm going back to the station right now to lock these spots into our system and consult with our production people."

W o r k s h e e t: How to Close Broadcast Sales Without Looking Like a Jerk

1. Rate the following closes relative to how often you use them. Use the number 1 for the close you use most often and 7 for the close you use the least.

_____ DIRECT CLOSE

_____ SUMMARY CLOSE

_____ ASSUMPTIVE CLOSE

_____ SRO CLOSE

_____ PEN CLOSE

_____ MINOR POINT CLOSE

_____ MAKE ME AN OFFER CLOSE

2. Write down any other closes that work for you on a regular basis.

CHAPTER
■■■ 24 ■■■

The Value of Super-Servicing Your Local Client

RELATIONSHIP SELLING AND HOW IT PAYS OFF TO HANG OUT WITH YOUR CLIENTS

Cardinal Rule: Neglected customers cancel. They do. It's a fact. If you don't stay in touch with the client you have on the air, you can bet that you'll get a call that says, "Cancel my spots." It's the client's way of saying, "You used to call me all of the time when you wanted my business. Now that you have it, you never call any more. So, I'm taking my ball and I'm going home."

Here's an example to consider. A church wanted to advertise a special Christmas event aimed at recruiting new members. I gave the minister the names of two account executives at two different stations. The minister called each account executive. One of them indicated that spot availability would be a problem. The other rep managed to work out a schedule. The minister tried several times to call the first AE to take what avails she had, but she wouldn't return his phone call. Too bad for her. He liked the results for the Christmas campaign so much that he's buying an annual contract from the station that took care of him. He says he will never do business with the rep who wouldn't return his calls. Although he's a preacher, he won't turn the other cheek to bad service. And he shouldn't.

After a seminar I did for clients, a man approached me and said, "I thought radio or television advertising didn't work. Now I know that my commercials were inundated with clichés. I was throwing crappy bait out there. Now I understand what my problem was." We talked for a while longer and he left, now convinced that it wasn't the stations he was using, it was the commercials. The next morning his account executive called. She said the client had just called her and chewed her out. I asked why. She said he asked her if she knew about clichés in advertising before she'd invited him to the seminar. She responded to him that, yes, she was aware of them. "Then, why didn't you tell me?" asked the client. Her response to him was, "I didn't think it was my job." Shame on her. Of course it's her job to make sure that the client is casting the best possible bait. She was either unfamiliar with how to write a good spot or just too lazy to bother to educate her client.

Aren't you sick of bad service? Waiters can't get your order right. The cleaners mess up your clothes. The clerk at the convenience store is talking on the cell phone, oblivious to the fact that the line is getting longer. When you thank someone you've just spent money with, instead of saying, "You're welcome," he says, "No problem." Well, it shouldn't be a problem. It's his job. Nobody seems to really care about the customer these days. But we're different in broadcast sales, aren't we? Unfortunately, no. In many cases, we're just as bad as any other service-oriented industry.

Clients have plenty of stories about horrible broadcast sales service. "I never see the (expletive deleted) unless he's trying to sell me something." Or, "She promised me she'd come back with a good idea, then I never saw her again." Or, "They ran the wrong copy for two months. I called and they said they'd change it, but they never did." Or, "All they ever do is ask me if I'm doing anything with them this month." Or, "They send me a new salesperson every six months. I'm sick of training broadcast salespeople."

Client service means so much more than just writing up an order and picking up a check. The bottom line is this: As a broadcast sales representative, it is your job to educate your clients and make sure their advertising dollars are spent as efficiently and effectively as possible. It is your job to make sure that their copy is well written and not just wallpaper clutter. It is your job to help your clients overcome marketing problems. It is your job to stay in touch with your clients and help them grow their businesses. It is your job to identify and solve as many problems as you can for them. This is how you get into the client's "circle of trust."

TAKE CARE OF CLIENTS PROPERLY AND THEY'LL PERCEIVE YOU AS A RESOURCE

By educating your clients properly and by identifying and solving problems they have, they perceive you as a resource instead of a pest. When it looks like you know what you're doing, you have more control and the client is more likely to listen to you, trust you, and confide in you, just as he or she would listen to, trust, and confide in his or her accountant, doctor, or lawyer. In other words, by gaining the client's respect, you avoid the tail wagging the dog syndrome.

People like to do business with someone they like and trust. There is no reason why your local direct clients shouldn't like and trust you. They would if you treated them as well as you'd treat a valued friend. That means taking care of business and being their advocate at your station by:

- Making sure that their copy is well written and that production gets handled in a timely and professional way.

- Making sure that their orders are entered correctly, with the fairest possible rates and good times.

- Making sure that their invoices are correct and sent in a timely fashion.

- Making sure that they have access to you, even after business hours, if they need you.

But nowadays, good service just isn't enough. You must strive to provide exemplary customer service. What do I mean by exemplary service? Identifying and solving customer problems, regardless of whether they're related to their advertising/marketing situation. In other words, just help people solve problems. The client will remember your generosity and it will come back to you tenfold.

Here are some examples.

- A tutoring service asked me for creative help. We became friends. The owners of the tutoring business had some internal management issues. They weren't getting along very well. They asked me to moderate a discussion to attempt to solve some of their problems. I did. It helped. Now they trust and respect me even more.

- A florist told me she never had enough drivers to deliver her arrangements on Valentine's Day. I offered to help her make the deliveries. I still do it. Not one single other vendor bothered to help her on her busiest day of the year. She loves me for that.

- I had an office supply shop as a client. I helped out during its busiest day of the year, the annual pen show. I caught a thief stealing a $300 pen. They still talk about that. I was a hero to that business. I also offered to speak at a few weekly sales meetings. I talked about selling. I talked about the strategy of our advertising campaign. They loved it. In fact, I was the only vendor they invited to their Christmas party. I declined. I told them I'd rather be the bartender, and I controlled the tempo of that Christmas party. We all had a blast.

- I had a car dealer client for years. Although it had an agency, I kept the account direct. The agency hated me, but I didn't care. I did things for the client that the out-of-town agency never even thought about. I invited him and his family to our home for parties, and I did sales meetings for him as well. The client and I are still friends. He trusts me implicitly, and I trust him.

EXEMPLARY SERVICE

This is what I'm talking about when I say exemplary service. Maybe you should get more involved in the lives of your clients. Why not? You're going to hang around with somebody, including people you work with. You spend some work time with your clients, so why not spend a little personal time and have the reputation for exemplary client service? Do something extraordinary for your clients. Be there for them all of the time, not only when they need you. If you learn something new or different that would benefit your clients, don't just sit on it, let them know what you've discovered and how it might be of use to them.

W o r k s h e e t: The Value of Super-Servicing Your Local Client

Think of three familiar local direct clients. From what you know about these businesses, write down a few ways you could provide extra service for these clients that would make you stand out from other media account executives.

CHAPTER

■■■ 25 ■■■

Collecting—How to Make Sure You Don't Work for Free

D
o you enjoy working for free? Think about all of the time and effort you put into getting a new account on the air. You prospected, you found the decision maker, you got an appointment, you made a presentation, you answered some tough objections, you came up with a creative idea, you scheduled production, you wrote up all of the paperwork to get the account scheduled. That's a lot of work. And now you find out you're not getting paid for that work? Bummer.

When somebody owes you money, you always look like the bad guy when he doesn't pay. This is so unfair. Collection takes up a lot of time that you could be spending developing new client business. And it seems like it's always the most difficult clients to work with that become the biggest collection problems.

We get greedy sometimes in broadcast sales. We are so desperate for the billing that we write up an order from a client without asking for cash in advance because the client bullies you into it. Even though we have a nagging feeling that we might encounter a collection problem, we still write up that business. And then, sure enough, you have to become a bill collector.

Bill collection isn't pleasant. It takes up a lot of your precious time. The collection process usually takes much longer than the original selling process. People who owe you money don't like to return your phone calls. They don't want to see you when you visit them. It seems like overnight their attitude toward you changed. They used to be nice, but now they treat you like an enemy. Why? You did nothing wrong. Why do they treat you like it's your fault that they can't pay their bill? It's nonsense.

Maybe we'd have fewer collection problems if we just followed our instincts and didn't take on risky business to begin with. Or, we could avoid collection problems altogether by always insisting on cash in advance. This chapter is designed to help you maximize your collection efforts and minimize future collection problems.

Nine ways to immediately improve collections at your station.

1. **Never let a collection problem go more than 24 hours before you take action.** The time to get busy with a collection problem is immediately upon discovering that the problem exists. More than thirty days with no payment from a new client is reason enough to become very concerned. The longer you wait to take action, the colder the trail becomes. To confirm that you actually have a problem, first give the client the benefit of the doubt. Call the client and ask if he or she received your invoice. If the client responds that he did not receive your invoice and you know that the invoice did in fact go out, then the client could be lying and you've got a collection problem. Offer to hand-deliver a duplicate invoice immediately in exchange for full payment.

2. **Keep in mind that if the client owes you money, he probably owes money to fifteen other vendors as well.** And you will be competing with those fifteen vendors for any dollars that the client does have. The old adage "the squeaky wheel gets the grease" definitely applies here. This means that you will have to make your collection calls

frequently and very personally if you are going to get the client's attention and your money.

3. **Always accept partial payment.** If the client tells you that he cannot pay the entire balance, ask what he can pay immediately. Obviously, offer to take cash. I've actually run into account executives who were offered cash but refused to take it saying, "We only accept checks." Stupid. Take the cash and write the client a receipt. Make certain the client signs a receipt that you can take back to the station with you.

4. **Set up a payment schedule.** Write up a payment agreement with installments over as many weeks as it will take for your client to pay the balance. Make it a contract with a place for you and your client to sign and date. Each time you come to collect your installment, ask the client if he or she could pay a little more this week.

5. **Be diligent.** Remember that it is a psychological fact that people who owe you money will not contact you. They will avoid your phone calls and your visits, if they can. So, if you can get through to the client, make certain that he or she understands that you have bills to pay as well and that you were depending on your commission from this transaction to help pay your bills. Communicating things that personalize your situation and make you stand out from the other creditors increases your chances of getting paid first instead of last, or not at all.

6. **Get every client's cell phone number early in the sales process.** If your client has a gatekeeper or secretary who always screens calls, you'll have trouble getting through with a collection problem. People are much more likely to answer their mobile phones. Call the mobile phone from a number that is unfamiliar to a client, and he'll probably answer it.

7. **Avoid collection problems altogether by always asking for cash in advance.** As a rule, bars, restaurants, manufactured home dealers, and promoters should always pay cash in advance, no matter what. There is no reason to assume

that every one of your clients automatically qualifies for credit. Although, incredibly, we usually offer credit instead of asking for cash in advance. What harm is there in asking for cash in advance with every single new direct customer? You're not a bank. You're a salesperson at a broadcast station. After closing a direct sale of any kind, tell the client matter-of-factly that you need to pick up a check before the schedule begins. If the client vehemently objects, you can bet that you will probably have a collection problem at some point in the future.

8. **Charge it.** Does your company accept credit cards? If so, suggest that the client put the balance owed on his or her credit card. Tell him he can earn points or mileage that way. Once this is done, your collection problem is finished. You are paid and it's now up to the credit card company to collect.

9. **Trust your instincts.** "If it smells like a fish, it's a fish." If you have an inkling of a feeling that you're going to get burned, don't write up the order until you get cash in advance. Otherwise, you'll probably wind up working for free.

W o r k s h e e t: Collecting—How to Make Sure You Don't Work for Free

1. Identify any client who is more than 45 days delinquent in paying your bill.

2. Based on what you've learned in this chapter, write down a definite course of action you'll take within the next seven days to resolve each delinquent account.

CHAPTER

■■■ **26** ■■■

How to Overcome Call Reluctance

Even though it's illogical, given the nature of our business, every salesperson at one time or another experiences a phenomenon called call reluctance. Call reluctance means exactly what it says, that, for some reason, you are simply reluctant to make client calls. In other words, you just don't feel like getting in the car or picking up the telephone to contact clients.

Call reluctance is the single biggest obstacle in getting more local direct accounts on the air. It's not our ratings. It's not our price structure. It's not the other stations. It's not the program or the format. It's not the economy. Those are just the excuses. The single biggest reason we're not billing more local direct on our stations is that we're not getting out of the station and calling on accounts.

In this chapter we'll discuss effective ways to deal with call reluctance. If you're struggling with making calls right now, this lesson will help get you off your rear end and back out on the street where you belong. If you haven't experienced call reluctance, this section will help you recognize the signs and save you time and money should it ever happen to you. And chances are it will. Watch out for it, because call reluctance tends to sneak up on you.

For some sellers, call reluctance is a way of life. Some salespeople would rather spend a day doing anything other than making in-person sales calls to local direct accounts. So they invent other things to keep themselves busy. This is called busywork.

DON'T CONFUSE EFFORT WITH PRODUCTION

In this business, if you've stopped calling on new clients, that means one of two things. Either you are doing so well that you don't have another waking minute to call on one more client (congratulations!), or you're in big trouble. And, you're in trouble if you'd rather sit in front of the computer, visit with the people down the hall, or go shopping than call on customers.

How can any of those thousands of businesses in your signal coverage area do business with you if you're not out there teaching them who you are, what you do, and how to get in touch with you?

HOW ARE YOU SPENDING YOUR DAY?

What's your daily routine? Do you have a daily plan? It's amazing how many sellers don't. Here's a routine with no road map. Do you know a few people like this?

"I get to the office at 8 or 8:30, okay, 9 in the morning. It's not my fault I'm late. The traffic is terrible. First, I go to the coffee machine. I can't work without my coffee. I run into a coworker. We discuss the game or *Desperate Housewives* or something else we saw on tv last night. After coffee I go to the restroom and then go back to the break room for another cup. Hey, it's time for a cigarette break. I need to smoke when I'm working. And Bill and Susan are out there. Okay, time to check the email. Lots of jokes to read and delete. I make a few obligatory client phone calls. Have to. The boss wants us to make a couple of calls. I might as well go home for lunch. Oh, yeah. Better stop at the cleaners and . . . is that new store finally open? Shopping here is fun. Oh no. What time is it? What happened to the time? I have the attention span of a *ferret on crack*. I'd better hurry back to the station. Man, it's already two in the afternoon. I'd better get back to the computer to crank out some crappy computer-generated proposals for clients. The clients won't understand them; heck, I don't even understand them. They'll probably reject them anyway. But these are really for the boss. The boss has been on me lately because my billing is down and suddenly she needs to see proof that I'm really working. Of course I'm really working. It's not my fault the economy is down. Besides, our station sucks in the ratings. Ooh, a message from that furniture client. Says it's important. Better call him back. No, that would be a bad idea. He's probably mad at me because I didn't call him yesterday. If I call him now, he'll probably cancel. Well, it's five o'clock anyway. Better start shutting it down for the day. Don't want to miss Happy Hour. Man, this media business sure is hard work. I deserve a drink. I wonder how long they'll keep paying me for this. Thank God I'm still getting a salary against commissions."

REASONS FOR CALL RELUCTANCE

- **Burnout.** You feel overworked and you feel you need a break. Solution—take a vacation. It will adjust your attitude.

- **Personality.** You just don't enjoy meeting new people. Solution—get another job where you don't have to interact with as many people.

- **Fear of rejection.** You hate hearing "NO." Solution—Change the way you ask for an appointment or change your pitch. If the way you're doing it now isn't working, try something new.

- **Dirty little secret.** Clients intimidate you because you are afraid you don't know what you're doing. Or, you made a promise to a client you never kept. Maybe you have a problem staying focused on the client and her business or some other issue. Solution—Apologize and make amends immediately. The longer you wait, the harder it gets. Own up to your mistake, determine what you need to do to correct it, and then take action. The sooner you do it, the better you and your client will feel.

- **Poor work habits.** You're getting sloppy and/or lazy. Solution—It's time to change bad habits and get back in gear.

Ten ways to improve your attitude and overcome call reluctance.

1. **Avoid negative self-talk.** Psychologist Abraham Maslow once said, "I can feel guilty about the past, apprehensive about the future, but only in the present moment can I act. The ability to be in the present moment is a major component of mental wellness." This quote is absolute gold. Memorize it like I did and watch bad days disappear. Teach yourself to ignore that little voice inside your head that tells you that you will fail. Refuse to dwell on guilt from the past or worry about the future. You have no control over events from the past. You can't accurately predict the future. All you really have control over is right now. Logically, anguishing about something from the past or fearing the future is a complete waste of time. You must stay focused in the present moment, which is really the essence of your life. Sometimes a good vacation is all you need to get you motivated again.

2. **Discipline yourself to make more calls.** Get your rear end out of that chair, away from the computer, and force yourself to make some calls. Take a look at the white business pages of your phone book and get a good idea of how many businesses there are in your market. Keep in mind that in an average month a typical radio station will have fewer than fifty direct accounts on the air. This means that most of the businesses in your area have never been called on properly, or have never been called on at all, and that means tremendous opportunities for those who bother to just make the calls.

3. **Distance yourself from negative people, office gossip, and any other negative conversation.** Refuse to participate. Negativity spreads like a virus. Avoid the Three Cs: Try not to *criticize, condemn,* or *complain.* Remember that you can change your internal operating system. You can choose to replace your negative thoughts with positive ones. When you catch yourself thinking negatively, consciously bring yourself back into the present moment and focus on something positive. You have to do this. Practice it. Make this part of the person you are or the person you are becoming. You've heard the phrase "to change your world, change your mind."

4. **Change the way you think about your closing ratio.** I always believed that the old adage, "call on ten, get three appointments, close one sale" seemed bleak. So I changed my closing ratio to nine out of ten. Here's what I mean. If I believe that I can help a client and that the client has the resources to allow me to help, I'll close that client eventually. Maybe not today, maybe not tomorrow, maybe not this quarter. But sooner or later, sometime this year, I'll close that sale.

5. **Stop schlepping spots and start educating clients.** Stop selling generic spot packages and get back to doing custom proposals and educating clients properly. Educated clients buy more than uneducated clients. Most direct clients know very little about the overall marketing process and much less about advertising, the strengths and weaknesses of different media, the difference between a good spot and a bad spot, or how to calculate return on investment from a media campaign. Think of yourself as a teacher instead of a salesperson.

6. **Expand your vision.** Instead of ganging up on the same direct clients that everybody else in town is calling on, go out into neighborhoods you rarely frequent and call on clients

who are unlikely to have been contacted by other stations and other media. As we discussed in Chapter 1, go hunting.

7. **Every time you make a call, you get paid.** What is your average sale when you do close a deal? What is your commission on that sale? What is your true closing ratio? Divide your closing ratio into your commission from an average sale and you'll realize that every time you make a new business call, it's like putting X number of dollars in your pocket. How much money do you want to make today? Make the calls and make the money.

8. **Don't give up.** If you come up with a brilliant campaign for a client and she doesn't buy it, don't just shelve the idea. Pitch a similar idea to everybody else in that product category until you sell it. If it's a really good idea, somebody will buy it.

9. **Deal with dirty little secrets.** Sometimes you won't make a call on a particular account because you are experiencing guilt regarding an issue with that client. Usually it's something minor. Deal with it. If the client deserves an apology, then do it, make the necessary amends and move on. You'll immediately feel better. Do it and get it over with.

10. **Change your pitch and get more appointments.** To get a meeting with a prospective client, use a headline to break through the clutter. "I just wanted to take a few minutes to talk about your advertising" just doesn't cut it any more. A better way would be to use an immediate attention-getting device, just like we do when we write a spot.

Ask yourself these questions: Am I spending enough time prospecting? If not, why not? Am I a member of a business leads group? Do I regularly get out of the office and go hunting for new local direct business? Am I slacking off because I see others getting away with it? What am I really doing with my precious time? Does it make logical sense?

Identify and correct attitudinal problems. If you're not making calls, then you're not making money. That's illogical. Who do you do business with, and have you ever talked to them about what you can offer? There are a lot of people out there that are willing to talk to you about what you can do for them, but they can't learn from you if you don't call on them.

Get busy now.

W o r k s h e e t: How to Overcome Call Reluctance

1. All salespeople experience call reluctance at one time or another. Identify your reason(s) for not making calls by marking the check box.

   ☐ **Poor work habits.** You're getting a little lazy. It's time to change bad habits and get back in gear.

   ☐ **Burnout.** You feel overworked and you feel you need a break.

   ☐ **Personality.** You just don't enjoy meeting new people.

   ☐ **Fear of rejection.** You hate hearing "NO."

   ☐ **Dirty little secret.** You are intimidated by a client because you are afraid you don't know what you're doing. Perhaps you made a promise to a client you never kept.

   ☐ **Other reasons.**

   _____

   _____

   _____

2. What steps will you take immediately to overcome call reluctance?

3. Identify two new prospects you have meant to call for some time, but haven't.

CHAPTER
■■■ 27 ■■■

Conclusion

It would seem logical to say that the last decade has brought more changes to the broadcast industry than we've be seen in the previous seventy years combined. Consolidation, technology, indecency issues, our relationship with advertising agencies, and competition from new media seem to have forever altered the broadcast sales landscape. Some of us are having a very difficult time adapting to new scenarios. That's too bad, because there is little you can do other than accept them and focus on new opportunities along with new challenges. Let's hope that you're one of those individuals who can embrace change quickly and can see the opportunities that new situations can bring your way.

Broadcasters are not strangers to change, and so far we have learned to adapt pretty well. Remember that not so many decades ago, radio salespeople had to accept the fact that they would lose audience (and advertisers) to a new upstart medium called television. Later, radio broadcasters had to accept that with the invention of the eight-track tape deck, they no longer had an in-car monopoly. Television sellers had to adapt to the intrusion of VCRs, computer games, cable, and satellite. Technology will always present challenges and at the same time, tremendous opportunity for those of us who can adapt.

As we in broadcast strive to stay relevant in our little sea of change, imagine the changes our local direct clients must be dealing with. More and more, local business owners are being eaten for lunch by national competitors as they try to fight back the only way they know how, with price. You know this is the worst defense for a local business. It is virtually impossible to win a long-term price war with a national discount competitor, but watch them as they try.

Local direct clients and local broadcast stations are made for each other. We fit each other like a glove fits your hand. The local direct client needs to reach the audience that we provide. We need long-term local direct business in order to survive. In a perfect world it would be easy. Local businesses, realizing how important broadcast stations are to their overall success, would call us and we would never have to call them. We would just sit by the phone and wait for the calls.

Fortunately for us in sales, it is not a perfect world. Station owners and managers appreciate the need for good media salespeople because local businesses typically don't call the stations looking to advertise. Instead, we must call them.

If you are smart about the way you approach broadcast sales, you understand that your competitors include the other sellers at your station. How you prospect for new business is critical to your success or failure. The first words you speak to a new prospect will be critical to whether you get an appointment. Your presentation skills and ability to listen will be critical in whether the client perceives you as a problem-solving resource or just another chiquita pest. Your game plan (or lack of one) will determine whether you wind up with a client who stays loyal to you for many years or a client who won't give you the time of day. Your ability to close long-term business will determine whether you will make a small fortune in this business or whether you'll ultimately quit or get fired. If you're going to play this game to win, you'll get there faster if you know what you're doing. You may have heard, "Life is hard, but it's a lot harder if you're stupid."

It's really all up to you. Armed with the right tools, an emphatic, ego-driven individual can write his or her own ticket to success in a very exciting chapter of the media and entertainment business. It is my sincere hope that this book will help you succeed in broadcast sales and that our paths might someday cross. Until then, good selling and best of luck out there, my friend.

Index